ROUTLEDGE LIBRARY EDITIONS:
WOMEN IN SOCIETY

I0127894

Volume 17

WOMEN'S PARTNERSHIP IN THE NEW WORLD

WOMEN'S PARTNERSHIP
IN THE NEW WORLD

MAUDE ROYDEN

Routledge
Taylor & Francis Group

LONDON AND NEW YORK

First published in 1941 by George Allen & Unwin Ltd

This edition first published in 2025
by Routledge
4 Park Square, Milton Park, Abingdon, Oxon OX14 4RN

and by Routledge
605 Third Avenue, New York, NY 10158

Routledge is an imprint of the Taylor & Francis Group, an informa business

British Library Cataloguing in Publication Data
A catalogue record for this book is available from the British Library

ISBN: 978-1-032-87216-2 (Set)
ISBN: 978-1-032-86826-4 (Volume 17) (hbk)
ISBN: 978-1-032-86859-2 (Volume 17) (pbk)
ISBN: 978-1-003-52964-4 (Volume 17) (ebk)

DOI: 10.4324/9781003529644

Publisher's Note
The publisher has gone to great lengths to ensure the quality of this reprint but points out that some imperfections in the original copies may be apparent.

Disclaimer
The publisher has made every effort to trace copyright holders and would welcome correspondence from those they have been unable to trace.

This book is a re-issue originally published in 1941. The language used and views portrayed are a reflection of its era and no offence is meant by the Publishers to any reader by this re-publication.

Women's Partnership

in the

New World

by

Maude Royden, C.H., D.D.

LONDON

George Allen & Unwin Ltd

FIRST PUBLISHED IN 1941

PRINTED IN GREAT BRITAIN
in 11-Point Baskerville Type
BY UNWIN BROTHERS LIMITED
WOKING

Contents

Preface

MEN have now given us the recognition we asked for. That we have equal status with them yet no one but the blind will affirm, but that we have a great deal more power than our foremothers had is certain. If we are to use it to the full, we must know something of our own past history—it is a longer one than twenty-two years!—and learn to know ourselves. The world is in a tragic mess. No nation, sex or class can put it right alone; but everyone must ask himself and herself what he and she can do in the building up of a world that will make even the agony and struggle of war seem worth while. To no section of any community does the need of a better life appeal more strongly than to women. Let us do our part.

Chapter I

Introductory

WOMEN are newcomers in public life. Most of them
have not arrived yet. If we are asked, as we often are,
why we have not yet turned the world upside down,
established universal peace among the nations and put
right every wrong, this is our answer.

Women in no part of the world are considered to be
the equals of men. They themselves almost everywhere
accept this estimate of their own value. In this country
and in many others, however, they are held to have
some worth, and lately—but only very lately—have
been given a good deal of freedom. The political vote
was won only twenty-two years ago* in Great Britain,
a little later in the United States, a little before or
a little after in some other countries.† But as the human
race is probably a million years old, twenty-two years
is not a great while in which to set right everything
that has been set wrong.

Now, however, though far from having real equality
with men even in this country, we are much freer and
more influential than we were, for example, during
the last or any previous century.

What are we to do with our freedom?

What special gifts have we with which to serve our
country and the world?

* February 1918. I write in 1940.

† In some it has already been lost again owing to the overthrow
of democracy, but this is true for men as well as women.

Women's Partnership in the New World

We have not done much yet, and we certainly have not had much time to do it in; but what we have done gives us some light on both these questions. We have indulged in no "anti-man" legislation such as some of the more panicky opponents of the granting of votes to women expected. We may defy these critics —and they are both male and female—to point to a single law passed by women over the heads of men and expressive of sex-antagonism. No such law has been passed or even proposed.

What has been done has been just what might have been expected.

From the first, women have felt a passionate interest in international peace. They have not abolished war —an institution probably as old as mankind—even in twenty-two years. They have, however, tried so hard to do it that workers in the cause of peace have, some-times in private, occasionally even in public, lamented the tendency of women to "swamp" men in the various peace societies.

Next to this, or equal to it, has been their interest in the welfare of children and the protection of the home. Their list of reforms has therefore included the protection of both girls and boys from too early mar-riage; from seduction by vicious persons, and this too for boys as against women as well as for girls against men.* The Guardianship of Infants, the Matrimonial Causes Act, the Widows, Orphans and Old Age Pen-sions Act of 1925, the Registration of Midwives, of Nurses and of Maternity Homes, the regulation and

* *Our Freedom and its Results,* edited by Ray Strachey, page 203. This book gives an excellent account of the progress of women and of their achievements since entering into public life.

Introductory

limitation of the employment of children and young people, the adoption of children, the protection of illegitimate children, and an Act forbidding the passing of the death sentence on a pregnant woman*—these are not spectacular performances, and few—probably none—would be opposed by any man to-day. They were, however, *passed* by the urgency and pressure of women.

The women of this country have not forgotten the existence of other countries within our sphere of influence. When the new constitution for India was being hammered out at Round Table Conferences in London, they insisted, both in Parliament and outside, on the right of Indian women to political power, co-operating in this demand with the small but brilliant group of Indian women who were sent here for the Conference. The age-old tragedy of the child slaves of Hong-Kong, tolerated by men who loudly claim that slavery does not exist under the British flag, has been dragged to light and what we hope is at least the beginning of the end of it brought about by the unceasing efforts of a woman Member of Parliament.† In this country and all the others in which women have entered public life progress has been in the same direction. Nothing is more noticeable both in national and international conferences where women meet together in discussion than this community of interest. Better housing, purer food, unadulterated milk, a greater emphasis on the value of the child, of the home, of the school, of the

---

* Affiliation Orders Act 1918, Bastardy Act 1923, Legitimacy Act 1926, Illegitimate Children (Scotland) Act 1930. See *Our Freedom and its Results*, pp. 44–51.

† Edith Picton-Turbervill, O.B.E.

rights of mothers—these have been the concern of women. There has been nowhere any sex-antagonism, but a change of emphasis, an increase in the interest shown in certain sides of life.

It is a modest beginning, but it shows the way which we women tread. What of the future?

It must bring far greater services to the world than these, but they will probably not be of a different kind. There is nothing to be afraid of, much to hope. Or rather, there *is* something to be afraid of, and it is this: that women will not recognize their own power, and so will fail to rise to the full height of their responsibility.

We are said to be more emotional than men and, like other generalizations about our sex, this is regarded as a reproach. But why? It is our strength that we are so. For it is not thought but emotion that drives the world. One may *think* a thing to be wrong and do nothing about it, or right and do nothing about it: one cannot *feel* it to be right or wrong without action. We know there are millions of people suffering from poverty that is actually destitution. So long as we do not see them we endure it, even with complacency, because though we know of their sufferings we do not feel them. Let one starving child be put before our eyes, and we do feel it. Our emotions are roused, and we act. Observe further that the emotion is a good one, and so is the act.

I am not quite sure that women are more emotional than men, but I hope they are, for, if they are, their influence in the future will be a driving force for lack of which the world of to-day is sick. People who are called "intellectuals" have thought and written and talked themselves out of breath and out of heart. One

Introductory

of the most brilliant of them, Mr. H. G. Wells, describes his experience. He puts, he tells us, a case of overwhelming logic before a deeply interested audience. He states the case for far-reaching changes in a social system about which all agree that far-reaching changes are what it needs. All are concerned, all are interested. As soon as he sits down a lively discussion begins. After a time the chairman points out that it is tea-time, and "everything stops for tea."

Mr. Wells demands to know *why* "everything stops" not only for tea but for ever. The answer is that everything stops, everything waits, because no emotion has been aroused.

Again and again I have heard this question put. Sometimes the speaker answers it himself. Rarely indeed does he realize that the only true answer lies in the fact that even men are not moved by logical conviction but by emotion. He would be ashamed to admit the truth of this. If he has the candour to do so, he does it with scorn. He refuses to appeal to people's emotions, and thinks himself right and even noble to refuse. He despises the speaker who does it and accuses him of "sob-stuff."

If on the other hand he *can* move the emotions of his hearers, and has sense enough to know that he had better do it if he wants to get anything done, he feels that he is flattering them if he pretends to do nothing of the kind. Mark Antony was not the first nor will Lord Baldwin be the last to get a move on by assuring his hearers that he did not, he could not, he would not appeal to anything so base as emotion.

> "I am no orator, as Brutus is;
> But, as you know me all, a plain blunt man,

Women's Partnership in the New World

> That love my friend; and that they know full well
> That gave me public leave to speak of him.
> For I have neither wit, nor words, nor worth,
> Action, nor utterance, nor the power of speech,
> To stir men's blood: I only speak right on;
> I tell you that which you yourselves do know,
> Show you sweet Caesar's wounds, poor poor dumb
>   mouths,
> And bid them speak for me: but were I Brutus,
> And Brutus Antony, there were an Antony
> Would ruffle up your spirits, and put a tongue
> In every wound of Caesar, that should move
> The stones of Rome to rise and mutiny."*

Such was Shakespeare's description of one of the most glorious appeals to emotion ever made. It was a mixture of good and bad emotion, but it worked because, whether good or bad, it was to the emotions that it appealed.

What could be sillier than this contempt for the emotions? If men and women can really only be moved by an appeal to the heart, and appeals to the head leave them unmoved, why regard this as a piece of wickedness? There is something imbecile in this contempt. If women are more emotional than men, it only means that they are more alive. Is that a thing to be ashamed of? The dead do not feel. We are alive, and we do feel. That is all that is implied by saying that we are emotional.

It is only a fear of being conceited that makes me hesitate to claim (not to admit, but to *claim*) that women are more emotional than men. I should be proud to claim it, but I think probably it is not true.

* *Julius Caesar*, Act III, Scene 2.

Introductory

What is true is that women should neither despise nor pretend to despise their sex for being emotional but should, on the contrary, proclaim the importance of the emotions and make us realize that without an appeal to them nothing will ever be done at all.*

Mark Antony appealed to both good and bad emotions. What our leaders should be on their guard against is not an appeal to the emotions but an appeal to base emotions. What our intellectuals should do is not to despise emotion but to teach us that a force of such immense power must be highly disciplined and wisely directed, for all power is dangerous.

The editor of a powerful newspaper was asked why he had such a warm spot in his heart for one of the most erratic and incalculable forces in a political world. He replied rather ruefully that he knew the politician referred to had no principles; "but he has such wonderful emotions." He had; and he got things done. If he had had principles as well, they would have been good things. As it was, they were a mixed bag.

It is often said, half admiringly, half ruefully, that "it is the women who get things done." It is true, because women are emotional. Yet men make wars and give all in making them. Why? Because they too are emotional! Because war appeals to the emotions and peace does not. When anyone dares to make peace as great an adventure as war he will abolish war. Gandhi has gone nearer to it than any man before him or now living in the world. He did not succeed by showing his followers that peace was more reasonable than war.

* For a most valuable discussion of this, read Professor John MacMurray's *Freedom in the Modern World.*

Women's Partnership in the New World

The place of the reason is to discipline and direct a highly dangerous and explosive force. This force is neither hysteria, sentimentality nor "*merely* feeling." It is, as its name implies, a *moving* force—an emotion. If men are really more reasonable than women, let them work together with us. They can make the engine: we will supply the steam.

Chapter II

Women and the Next Civilization

IN a world at war women will always be at a dis-
advantage, for wars are won by a combination of
spiritual power and physical violence and, though
equal in the first, women are not equal to men in their
use of the second.

It is absolutely necessary for women to recognize this
truth, for truth it is.

Women are equal to men in endurance, and may
even surpass them. I am inclined to think they do. In
violence they are not equal, and I believe they never
will be. It is true that modern weapons of war can in
some cases be wielded by women. A woman with a
machine-gun may be the equal of a man with a
machine-gun. A woman in a bombing aeroplane can
fly her machine and drop her bombs with as shattering
an effect as a man. The bombs will explode with equal
violence. But they would be very blind people who
imagined that, because this is so, women would be as
valuable as men on the battlefield, or that an army of
women equipped with the most up-to-date arms in the
world could hold their own against an army of men
equipped in the same way.

There is, in fact, a deep aversion in the hearts both
of men and of women from the thought of women
organized, as men are, for the mass murder of war. An
individual woman will in extremity seize a gun or any
other weapon that she can lay hands on to defend her

children, her home, her person, or the honour and safety of her country. History gives us many such heroic stories, and Joan of Arc is only the greatest among these many. Nevertheless the world is (I hope) no nearer to accepting the idea of an army of women soldiers, and the reason is found not merely in an inferiority of muscle, but in something much deeper. It is the feeling that women are meant to be the creators and not the destroyers of life: that a woman's body, being the gateway of life for every human being born into the world, should not become the means of death. This feeling is not sentimental. It is based upon a profound instinct, and that instinct is as strong in men as in women, in women as in men. I believe that a civilization which disregards it is doomed, for it would be disregarding something fundamental. But there is no such "civilization." Not even Russia, nor Germany, nor Japan, has armed its women on a large scale.* If they have not, it may safely be said that no one will.

Women, then, are the guardians of life. What does this mean?

It means that, in co-operation with the man, the woman conceives her children. In co-operation with the man. So she knows from the beginning that life depends on co-operation. The silly idea that conflict is the fundamental law of life is denied from the outset. It is not so. Love creates life, and without love life would soon cease.

When I say this, I find that there are always some nit-wits who will exclaim that not all parents love each other, that a child may be born of a rape, and that

* Only Russia, I believe, has created so much as a regiment or so of women soldiers.

20

Women and the Next Civilization

"modern science" (which is supposed capable of anything) can impregnate a woman and enable her to conceive a child without love having anything to do with the matter. Let it be granted—if anyone is interested. Let those who *are* interested reflect on the possibility of a whole nation, healthy and vigorous—that is to say, really *alive*—depending for its citizens on these methods, and they will see for themselves the imbecility of the argument. It is not worth considering. Let it go.

Nations will be living and vigorous in proportion as they reproduce themselves through the agency of men and women who heartily love each other, whether the love be primitive passion or the more civilized and complete union which is both passion, tenderness, and loyalty. The creative act must be the act of lovers, and that life arises from love is one of the laws of the universe. It is of the nature of God Himself.

> "In the beginning God created the heavens and the earth."*
> "God is Love."†

Women should find it easier than men to remember the necessary connection of life and love. A man may beget life and go his way and forget it. A woman who has conceived cannot do so. She is the guardian of that life. For nine months it is dependent on her and her alone. Moreover, she will find that she is actually compelled by nature, and without choice of her own, to put the child's life before hers. Whatever food she takes goes first to nourish it: what is left is hers. It is a fact that an under-nourished woman can bear a

* Genesis i. 1.   † 1 John iv. 8 and 16.

21

healthy and well-nourished child, and does so in hundreds of thousands of cases. Of course, if she gets too little even for the child to live on, it will suffer; but whatever she does get goes to it first.

This is a parable in itself. Nature teaches us from the very beginning of life that life depends on self-sacrifice and that love puts the beloved before itself.

When the child is born, it still depends on the physical resources of the mother and on her guardianship and care. Men and women sometimes quarrel about the sorts of work each should do or leave to the other to do, but so far men have not disputed the right of women to the care of young children, on which for so many years their very lives depend.

Here the human child shows a deep difference between itself and the young of other creatures. Even the highest animal takes no more than a few weeks or months before it is able to look after itself. The child takes long years of guardianship and support. The animal, once grown, no longer even recognizes its parents and the tie between them ceases to exist. The child not only takes much longer to be "grown up," but when its need of its parents for food and shelter is at an end, it is still bound to them by ties of affection and gratitude and still looks to them for protection and guidance. Insensibly, as the child grows to be a man or woman, the relationship changes and the parents become dependent on him, as he once was on them. The tie remains and is a real and living thing throughout life.

The husband has become a father, and the child owes as much to him as to his mother. In other words, the experience of woman teaches her from one end of

Women and the Next Civilization

life to the other that life depends on love and on the co-operation of all with each. A home is not complete unless there is in it a father, mother and child—or, let us say, children. Each has to play his part, each is necessary for the well-being of all. However many children there are, every child brings something to the rest of the family—if it is only a chance of learning patience and understanding! In a large family there is often, and especially among the poor where it is most needed, a touching kindliness and consideration of the older for the younger children. The baby is the pride and care of the family, the handicapped or "afflicted" is looked after with unfailing patience. And this is not in rare cases, but in the vast majority of homes and as a matter of course. This is, in fact, "human nature," and it is not bad but good.

The experience of women as bearers of children is as old as the human race. The making of homes came next.

At first, in many cases and perhaps all, human people wandered about and camped at different places every night. They still do that in some countries. A midwife who had worked in Tierra del Fuego told me that the inhabitants marched each day along river-banks, from camping-ground to camping-ground. If a woman has a child, she merely falls out of the ranks till it is born; severs the umbilical cord with her teeth; washes the child and herself in the ice-cold river; claps it on her shoulder and hurries after the main body. No one stays to help her, nor does she need help. She has performed a function as natural to her as any other, and is not a whit distressed or exhausted.

Let me add that this ease is not by any means shared

Women's Partnership in the New World

by all "primitive" women. Some of them suffer considerably in childbirth. However, the bearing of children is the universal experience of all women in a savage state and of the enormous majority of women everywhere. They create life, and they do not create it alone. The knowledge that the physical attraction and need of men and women for each other is the cause of procreation is rarely lacking and, if there is ignorance on the subject,* it is an ignorance which speedily vanishes with the advance of civilization or contact with civilized people.

As soon as possible, the woman who is a mother wants a home. She does not want to be perpetually on the march. Her influence, however unconscious, is all on the side of the settled life. Men may ask for nothing better than hunting, fishing and fighting, with intervals of feasting and sleeping. Women want something more. They begin to create a settled life. They occupy themselves with the household crafts. They are the humble beginners of agriculture and farming. These words sound all too grand for the facts, but they *are* facts nevertheless. As long as people only hunted and fought they could roam from place to place, and even *had* to do so to find their prey. If they were to cultivate the soil in even the most rudimentary way, they must stay put. He (or she) who plants will want to reap.

So the home began, and women liked it much better than the trail, and found it suited their children better too. Women therefore can claim that they are the real beginners of arts and crafts, the first agriculturists, the founders of home life. It is a proud boast, for these are

* Anthropologists say that there are savage peoples who do not know that sexual intercourse is the cause of conception.

Women and the Next Civilization

the things that make human beings human. Animals can hunt and fish and fight. They do. They have to. They do not get much further than that, but they do that, in most instances, superbly. It is when humans begin to live together in homes that the vast gulf that exists between them and the lower animals begins to open. It is then that the mind begins to develop. "God breathed into his nostrils the breath of [spiritual] life; and man became a living soul."*

This then is the background of woman's life all over the world: the settlement, the home. She can only be understood and rightly valued if this is always remembered. This place—the home—was created by her to meet the need of her children. Because they are so weak, so helpless, so long in growing up, they need a stable and a settled dwelling-place. She provided it, she created it. It has been said that "woman continues the creative work of God."† And also that "as God could not be everywhere, he created mothers." Both these sayings came from Frenchmen, and it is noticeable that in no country is the mother held in greater honour than in France, children more loved or family life stronger.

"Woman continues the creative work of God." This is really true. Women have far the greater part in the creation of human beings. When we realize this we see why they have not been great in the other "creations" of man—in art, in science, in invention.

Some people believe that when women are as free as men are‡ to have the education and training neces-

---

* Genesis ii. 7.
† "La femme continue l'œuvre créatrice." Author unknown.
‡ And that is not saying a great deal.

sary for creative intellectual work, they will excel in it equally with men. I do not expect it. I expect a few women here and there to excel: they have done so already and will do it more in the future because they will be freer. But human beings, even the greatest, have only a certain limited amount of vital energy, and if the great majority of women continue to bear and rear children—as they certainly will—they will not also create great works of art or make world-shaking scientific discoveries. We shall have a Sappho or a Marie Curie, but we shall not have them often. We shall have women who "continue the creative work of God" by bearing children, and we shall some day learn the great truth that to create a fine human being out of one's own flesh and blood is actually as remarkable and satisfying an achievement as to carve an Apollo out of marble or to extract radium from pitch-blende. These are great and glorious achievements. From a full heart I salute them. I glory in the knowledge that one of them—the discovery of radium—was the work of a woman, and a woman of such noble character, so self-regardless, so fine, so pure, as to make her one of the saints of science. Because such women exist I shall resent and denounce every attempt to dogmatize about "woman's sphere" or to deny to women complete freedom to decide for themselves what they shall attempt and what is within their powers. How poor the world would be without such women! How immeasurable its loss if there had never been a Marie Curie, a Catherine of Siena or a Joan of Arc!

To say this is not to unsay what I have said already. The vast creative energy of women will in the future

Women and the Next Civilization

as in the past continue to pour itself into the great channel of motherhood. The women artists, the scientists, theologians, will be more numerous because less hampered, less repressed than in the past; but they will continue to be in a very small minority compared with the number of men engaged in these creative tasks.

Sometimes, when I realize that some men are seriously jealous of the achievements of women in what they think is their own particular sphere, I long to reassure them. "Do not be anxious," I should like to say: "the more spectacular parts in the drama of life will continue to be reserved for you—if not without exception, still very nearly so. Women will continue to make *you*. Out of their own bodies, with their own flesh and blood, they will make you and glory in it. You will continue to give to us great works of art, great discoveries, great laws, great poetry, great books. Women will do so too—but not very often. You need not be jealous. Be as great and glorious as you can. The more glorious the better. The women who are your mothers will see of the travail of their souls and bodies and will be satisfied with it."

In the homes, however, and as mothers, the influence of women must now be weighed in the balance.

Inevitably it is a stable one. It arose out of the *settling* of men and women. Nothing like a home can exist until there is a possibility of staying in one place, at least for a time. No arts, no crafts can be practised. The soil cannot be cultivated. Even if women had not tried to do any of these things, the fact that they induced the wandering tribes to stay put would entitle them to be called the founders of civilization. Nomads

27

Women's Partnership in the New World

produce nothing. It sounds romantic to be a wanderer. There is no doubt that wandering is in the blood of some men and even of some women. They must be for ever on the move. If they are poor they will be tramps, if rich globe-trotters—or even, so insistent is their lust for wandering, globe-trotters without being rich. "I must go down to the sea again," they cry; or "take the golden road to Samarcand." Why not? It takes all sorts to make a world. Nevertheless, the great mass of men and women are nomads only if and when poverty compels them. Give them a fairly fertile soil, a secure position, and the possibility of making a livelihood where they are, and they settle down. Then and only then do they begin to produce. Food, better food, more varied food; better-built houses; warmer clothes. Then, if one is making or building for more than a night, it becomes worth while to make well and to build beautifully. What one makes well one loves, and what one loves one decorates.

Out of the settlement the home, and out of the home good work and beauty. The arts and crafts. Civilization.

This is the work of women. It is at once conservative —for its background is always settlement—and creative, for settlement alone makes creation possible.

Let women now be on their guard against the dangers of these admirable qualities. Their influence may be used not only for stability but for the arrest of natural and proper growth. When one's roots are struck deep into the soil it is easy to "get stuck" and to resent any attempt on the part of other people to move. It becomes difficult to believe that a move can be good, even when assured that it is a move forward; difficult

Women and the Next Civilization

to accept the assurance that one good custom can corrupt the world. It was not a woman who wrote:

"The old order changeth, yielding place to new,
And God fulfils himself in many ways,
Lest one good custom should corrupt the world."*

That has been too hard a saying for most women. Order has been so slowly and so hardly established that they cling to it with all the passion of creators for the thing they have created.

And the life in the home which belongs essentially to the home and does not look outside it has made the spirit of women as narrow as it is deep. Having established their homes, they were content to let men take the rest of the world. And men were well content with the division.

Outside their homes the influence of women was small and their interest hardly greater. It is not strange that this should still be the case. An artist is not expected to be a politician or a scientist to run a great business. It is enough that he should do his job, and the world owes him a great debt of gratitude for that alone. So with women. It is enough, we say, if a woman is a good wife and mother. If she puts her mind into her job she will find it big enough, and the world will not ask more of her.

It *is* a big job. It *is* a necessary one. The world does well to be grateful to women who do it well.

So they have concentrated on doing it well, and those whose lot it has been to grow up in a really good home know that it is as near to the kingdom of heaven on earth as the human race has yet reached.

* Tennyson, *The Passing of Arthur*.

Women's Partnership in the New World

Such a home is built true to the laws of life. Whole passages from the Sermon on the Mount are lived out day by day and hour by hour in such homes. The "old law"—that which was said "by them of old times"—is outworn here and left behind. Parents do not ask "an eye for an eye and a tooth for a tooth" when their children offend them, and they are only too ready to love the offender and to "go with him twain" when asked to go a mile. They do not think of justice but of love and make the sun of their love to shine upon the evil and on the good. The "counsels of perfection" of which the Sermon on the Mount is composed are commonplaces in thousands of homes, and no one is surprised to see them practised, especially by mothers. People who cross the threshold of such homes are set at ease almost without knowing it. They breathe freely and "make themselves at home."

What a lovely phrase! How vividly it makes us realize what "home" is, that the kindest wish of the kindest hostess should be expressed just like that! "Make yourself at home." All the bad homes in the world have not spoiled that wish for us or robbed us of its meaning. Even if we ourselves had no home worth calling a home, we know what it stands for; we are grateful, in a strange house, for all the wealth of kindness that is intended when we are bidden to be "at home."

Women have done that. This meaning of the word *home* is proof of what, with all the bad homes set in the balance, women have made the simple word *home* mean to mankind to-day. It is a great achievement. What it means for mankind in the future we have yet to see.

Women and the Next Civilization

Here I want to make clear the danger that exists in the very strength of women.

Property can hardly exist until one settles down. Even to-day, in this property-ridden world, those who travel much learn to travel light. I once travelled thousands of miles with a friend who carried all his belongings in two small—really small—bags. We were on a lecturing tour, and I learned that one of the bags was kept exclusively for books, papers, etc. I exclaimed with amazement, "Do you pack all your other belongings in *one* of those small bags?" "Yes," he said, looking at it ruefully, "and I am trying to see how I can do with less."

All good travellers do so. They are for ever seeing how they can do with less. When they stop, they begin to amass possessions, without which it now seems that they cannot live. Indeed, as has been seen, it is *because* people (women) want possessions that they gradually induce men to settle down; and out of these possessions they have created homes, towns, civilization.

How hardly shall they that have possessions make up their minds to pack what is necessary, discard what is not and—move on.

This is true of material things and material travelling. It is equally true of material things and spiritual travelling. There are homes, created by devoted wives and mothers, which have become spiritual prisons for husbands and children. A piano that must not be played, a carpet that can hardly be walked on, a room that is never or hardly ever used though the house is small and the other rooms crowded to the point of inconvenience, strained nerves and loss of temper—these are too often the sign of the "house-proud"

31

matron. The word "house-proud" has become a horror. It means that the house has become more important to the housewife than the people who live in it. It means that, for her, man was made for the house and not the house for man. Such a house has in fact ceased to be a home and has become a prison. One dare hardly move or breathe in it.

It is the outward and visible sign of a spiritual bondage.

Women are the conservative element in the race. They do not rush about, leaving most things behind and "making" nothing. They are the strength of our stability. But human beings cannot stay put for ever. They must leave things behind sometimes. At this point, too often, they find a dead weight of opposition in the women. Women, weighed down by possessions, cannot and will not move on. They say, "the old is better." While men incline to lose what they have through continually opening their hands to grab at something else, women lose what they might have through holding too tightly on to what they have got and refusing to open their hands at all. Thus "women are the conservative sex" has been said again and again and said truly.

Since we naturally suppose that our own country is highly civilized and progressive, we can see the truth of what I have said with clearer eyes when we look at other lands. The woman behind the purdah in India, those with bound feet in China, are said to be the real drag on the progress of the men and nation as a whole. It is they whose prejudices, inertia, obstinacy, are holding things back; they who, even in the matter of their own freedom, will not move. The Turkish

Women and the Next Civilization

"purdah" woman keeps her veil till it is removed almost by force.* The Chinese mother binds her daughter's feet; the Indian mother-to-be and her mother-in-law insist on the observance of superstitious rites and ceremonies in childbirth, which endanger the very lives both of mother and child. So we are told, and there is much truth in it. We have, however, equally obstructive examples of this unprogressive spirit among the women of our own country.

There are a terrifying number of women who resist with obstinacy the "growing up" of their own children. To them a child is a property—"something of my very own, for me to love." Husbands also are "something of my very own" too often, at least at the first. When they show signs of rebellion, they may be replaced by their own children. Here, at least, is something that the mother can surely call "her very own"!

I think of motherhood with reverence. I have quoted with the utmost accord the wonderful saying that "woman continues the creative work of God." Most of us, and men almost without exception, have a feeling for their mothers which, in respect and gratitude, sets them apart from all others. When a man refuses to fight he is asked "What would you do if an enemy attacked your mother?" It is the strongest plea of all, for there is a depth of feeling in a man's heart for his mother that differs from and perhaps even exceeds that for his wife or his child. Though not a man, I sympathize with this feeling of the unique character of the bond between a mother and the child, male or female, to

* Mustapha Kemal had to pass a law forbidding the veiling of women before he could induce them to forgo this suffocating form of bondage.

whom she has given birth. There is nothing deeper, nothing holier. It is unique.

Nevertheless—since "the corruption of the best is the worst"—I do not hesitate to say that the maternal instinct has often been a curse and mother-love a mere prison to its unfortunate object.

Do not be horrified at such strong language. It is the very strength and value of motherhood that is its danger, for every strength is dangerous and every strength has its weakness. When women made settled homes in which to bear their children, they immensely changed the whole manner of life of the human race. This not only shows the greatness of their power, but it proves that the power has been used in accordance with the real nature of man and with the fundamental laws of our being. Women could not have achieved such world-wide success if, in creating settled homes, they had been working *against* human nature—even male human nature. Unconsciously, women and men (together as always) accepted a way of living that was less animal, more truly and rightly human, than that which it left behind.

The proof of this lies in the world-wide acceptance of the change from the nomadic to the settled life. There are very few nomads left in the world to-day, and those are almost always nomads because they are poor, and roam from place to place to seek food, rather than nomads by choice.

But settlement and possession is almost the same thing. When we settle down we acquire possessions, or when we acquire possessions we settle down. It is much the same in the end. The home is woman's chief possession: and with the home go the children.

Women and the Next Civilization

When the children begin to grow up, they no longer "belong" to their mother. She has sacrificed everything for them, and yet they consider that they belong to themselves. This is hard to bear. It is literally true that each child is *made* by its mother, that is to say, its body is made out of her flesh and blood. How natural to feel that it is indeed "her very own"!

Mothers tell us that there is no companionship in life so close as that of a woman with her unborn child. As the child quickens, the mother realizes its separate and yet utterly dependent existence. It is a living creature. It can move—sometimes very disconcertingly!—without her telling it to do so. It is hers, and yet it is itself. I have known women who looked forward with a certain reluctance to the time when this strange and unique companionship must cease, the child leave her body, the cord be severed. They dread it, not because of the fear of labour, or perhaps I should say quite apart from the fear of labour; they dread it because it is the end of this strange companionship.

When the child is born, however, the mother still feels that it is in a sense a part of her. Just as a man, though he "leaves his father and mother and cleaves to his wife,"* still has for his mother an absolutely unique feeling, so has the mother for her child.

I asked one of the most devoted wives I ever knew whether she loved best her husband or her son. He was an only son, an only child. She hesitated for a moment, and then said that she had once had the frightful experience of having both husband and son dangerously ill in different and widely separated parts of England. She was with her husband, by what might

* Genesis ii. 24; Matthew xix. 5; Mark x. 7.

35

have been his death-bed, when she received a telegram to go at once to her son, who was to undergo a very dangerous operation. After an agonizing hesitation she decided to stay with her husband. "And so I suppose you will say," she commented, "that I loved my husband best. I don't know. Perhaps it was the fact that I was actually with him, and the journey to my son might have been useless, for he might have died before I reached him, that decided me. I don't know. I can only say that, though I did decide to stay with my husband, when I thought of my son dying I felt as though a limb was being torn from my body."

That expresses what I am trying to say. It is not a case of less or more love: it is a different love, and the bond between mother and child is like that of a limb to the body. That child was once part of her body. There can be no companionship *like* this, though there may be better.

Because there is no companionship *like* that of a mother and her unborn child, it is hard for her to believe that there can be a better. There is a child-bearing all over again for her, as the child of her body has to become a person, not now "her very own." For most women labour is a stern business. It is called "labour" because pretty nearly every muscle in her body comes into active and energetic use. And we speak of the "pains" that warn her that her hour is come, for they are pains indeed. I have seen children born, even in "civilized" countries, with little labour and almost without pain, but this is as rare as it is good. Generally speaking, the words "labour" and "pain" are only too appropriate. Yet the great mass of women stand up to them magnificently and, not only

Women and the Next Civilization

after the birth of the child but beforehand, so "forget the anguish"* that they desire it beyond everything and count their lives half wasted if it is denied them.

There are mothers wise enough and selfless enough to look forward without dread to the time when their children must cease to be mentally and spiritually dependent on them too. It cannot be an easy job. It means another travail, another anguish, before a child ceases to be a child and a human being is come into his own. I have often wished that the "schools for mothers" which are now so mercifully common could be followed up by a more advanced course! In the ante-natal clinic mothers are taught to look forward to their confinements without over-anxiety or fear and advised how to make the birth of their children as safe and easy for both as medical science and common-sense hygiene can make them. People do not realize how great a part the attitude of the mother plays in this regard. Students of midwifery, at a nursing-home at which I was a student, were often asked by the teacher, "What is the most important factor in a happy delivery?" And the answer was "a good mother." Not until I attended this nursing-home did I realize how true this was. The courage, intelligence and self-sacrifice of the mother is of high value for her child, even in the performance of a function which many people think of as purely physical. That courage is rarely lacking.

* "A woman when she is in travail hath sorrow because her hour is come: but as soon as she is delivered of the child, she remembereth no more the anguish, for joy that a human being is born into the world."—John xvi. 21. (The word usually translated *man* should be *human being*.)

37

Women's Partnership in the New World

But for the second bearing of a child, now to become not a child from a foetus but an independent human being from a child, there is singularly little preparation and few ante-natal clinics. All that mothers get, for the most part, is a scolding from that critical and self-appointed mentor, the "modern psychologist." It is rather like scolding young people when they marry in haste and find they have married the wrong person; for their error might quite often not have been made if wise counsel before marriage, instead of denunciation after it, had been available.

According to some "modern psychologists," a child would be lucky if it had no parents at all. Their influence is held to be purely mischievous, and the child better without them. But, setting aside these fanatics, we could learn a great deal and avoid many mistakes and many pangs if we listened to what the real student of human nature had to say. The psychologist is just that when he is wise.

If then we had an ante-natal clinic for mothers to help them through the often agonizingly difficult business of launching their children a second time into the world, we should not have so many possessive mothers, whose love for their children is at bottom no better than a love of possessions. Such love is one of the most destructive forces in the world. I say this deliberately and with a wide experience of the difficulties of young people.

There are some whose mothers will not let them go. They "spoil" them in a most literal sense. They want them to be for ever babies and do their best to keep them so. They pride themselves on "sacrificing everything" for their children. They "wait on them hand

Women and the Next Civilization

and foot." They never ask a service of any kind from their sons, but encourage them to be utterly selfish and utterly inconsiderate, if only they can at the same time make them entirely dependent on themselves. Then they—the mothers—sit back and pride themselves on being good mothers. They believe they *are* good mothers and they resent with extreme bitterness the "ingratitude" of the boy who at last breaks away and leaves home.

It is true that such women constantly say that they want nothing so much as a happy marriage for their sons. It is also true that in fact they cannot endure the thought of marriage at all and always find that the particular girl the boy wants to marry is the wrong one. The right one never appears.

Some mothers "promise" their sons—often before they are born!—"to God," by which they mean to the priesthood or ministry of religion. It is astounding that such unparalleled effrontery is often recorded with reverent admiration. "So-and-so's mother," we are told with hushed voice, "promised God that, if he would give her a son, she would dedicate him to the ministry."

Women often and justly complain that men have treated them as chattels. It would be difficult to imagine a more outrageous assumption of the rights of property than this "giving" of a hoped for son to a vocation for which he may be quite unfitted. In any case he has not been consulted before being offered up!

Daughters are even more commonly treated as property. Their right to live their own lives, though many people believe it now conceded, is very far from being established. Many parents decide, before they are born,

39

Women's Partnership in the New World

that they shall be boys and feel, what they seem to think they have a right to feel, resentment against the daughter because she is not a son. Psychologists have not yet made up their' minds whether and to what extent the state of mind of an expectant mother affects her child, but it is impossible to believe that it makes no difference at all. The imbecile habit of alluding to the child as "he" or "my son" will not bluff it into being a boy when it is a girl, and the mother who pompously announced to me "I have conceived a son" was delivered of a daughter notwithstanding; but is not this futile expectation a proof of the mother's determination to have what *she* wants, and to mould the life of her child even before it is born? It is probable that such a child suffers psychological hurt at the time: it is certain that it does so if the mother is unable—and she often is—to conceal her disappointment later on.

Such fantasies as calling a girl child by a boy's name, or an ambiguous one, cutting her hair in a boyish style, and even dressing her in boy's clothes,* are mercifully not very common; but the openly expressed disappointment which is quite common is hardly less damaging to a girl's self-respect and happiness.

I am not here concerned with the question whether parents are right in preferring boys to girls as they so often do. Some prefer girls to boys. My point is that the determination to have either one or the other, and the resentment felt (and expressed) when the "wrong" child appears, is a striking example of the possessive side of maternal love at the very outset.

"Love" of this kind is a real disaster. I have met some sons, and far more daughters, whose lives have

* Fortunately, not so very different from girls, nowadays.

Women and the Next Civilization

been poisoned by it. As sons are sometimes "dedicated to religion," so are daughters, much more commonly, "dedicated" to marriage. Marriage is the happiest life for most human beings, male or female, but not for all. There are born celibates of both sexes, and their being almost forced into marriage by anxious parents is a great wrong. Nor should they be deprived of an independent life, a career or a vocation, because their parents "want them at home." Sometimes (but by no means always) mothers whose daughters are in rebellion assure me that they, the mothers, "are not selfish." If a daughter wished to leave home in order to marry, they would not for a moment wish to stop her: it is only that any other motive for leaving "is so unnatural." And again the cry arises: "I did everything for her!" Sometimes, however, even marriage is forbidden or grudged to a useful daughter.

Such an unwarrantable claim on the life of another human being sets up a conflict in the mind of all but the strongest characters. This is where the poison enters. It is not that a daughter's (or a son's) "career" is always of the first importance: what matters is the resentment felt by any normal being against such a possessive claim. The fact that it is made in the name of motherhood makes it more bitter, for motherhood *is* a claim, and it is one most difficult to deny without inward self-reproach. There is a moral bullying here which the adolescent hates but which leaves him or her in a dilemma which often goes unsolved and frustrating through life.

Maternal love can be the purest and most selfless love on earth. It often is. When it is so, the mother passes through this second childbirth with glory. She

41

understands that it is at least as difficult for her child as for herself. "When we are born we cry that we are come to this great stage of fools."* Though Shakespeare wrote it, he put the saying into the mouth of a madman. Perhaps, with his vast knowledge of the human heart which made him a born psychologist, he would, had he been speaking for himself, have written "When we are born we cry with fear at this strange new world into which, willy-nilly, we are thrust." It is hardly stranger or more frightening to the babe who leaves the warm security of its mother's womb for a cold and perhaps a hostile world than for the adolescent boy or girl now looking beyond the home at "life." Yet youth is impelled, by a necessity as real as that which forces the baby out of the womb, to enter this new and large and frightening world. He—or she—needs all the courage he can call up to face this world, even while he desires to do so above all things. He should not have to face also the fear of disapproval and even condemnation from those who gave him life and com-pelled him to start on the dangerous career of being a human being. Like the expectant mother, the mother of the youth should prepare for his leaving her a second time. She should no more confine his adolescent mind in swaddling clothes than nowadays she dreams of confining his little baby body. She should be ready herself to sever the umbilical cord and should no more regret or resent this second separation than she did the first: or, if she must regret it, let her "forget the anguish for joy that a human being is born into the world."

We have yet a long way to go and psychologists yet an infinite amount both to learn and to teach. It is,

* *King Lear.*

Women and the Next Civilization

however, surely established that we must all grow up in more than our bodies. It is known that to refuse to do so is a most dangerous and subtle temptation—a tragedy if the refusal is maintained. Many of us who are now in years and appearance quite grown up are acutely aware of our own apparently incurable childishness. How we regret it! How discordant is the state of mind of one who is in some parts of his nature strong, brave and wise, and yet in others childish and savage! How paralysing is such discord! How difficult it makes us to live with, how unreliable, how disappointing!

Perhaps there is no man (I use the word as meaning *human being*) who is or ever has been quite undiscordant with himself because equally developed, equally mature in every part of him. For my part, it is because I find this quality of perfect and balanced maturity in Jesus Christ that I cry "Ecce Homo—Behold the Man!"* Not as Pontius Pilate did, but as countless millions of men and women have done since then—millions, among whom are many great saints, many geniuses, many conquerors of themselves, all aware that they have not reached this glorious humanity of the perfect Man because some part of them is still undeveloped, childish, savage. It is this natural and harmonious development that, as the years went by, marked Jesus of Nazareth as the perfect Human Being—the "increase in wisdom and in stature." He became the measure of the stature of the fullness of all God meant us to be.

> "Whom do men say that I, the Son of Man, am?"
> "Thou art . . . the Son of God."†

We are far indeed from this.

* John xix. 5.   † Matthew xvi. 13 and 16.

43

Women's Partnership in the New World

We are very primitive Christians still. It is said that the human race has existed, that is to say, it has been *human*, for half a million or a million years, and perhaps longer still. Christianity is not yet two thousand years old. Perhaps we ought not to be surprised that we are still so far from being Christlike. Still, there is something profoundly disappointing in the repeated failure of humanity to keep its foothold on the heights which civilizations have again and again reached. We look with miserable disappointment at the ruins of the great civilizations of the past. We learn from ancient records of the heights that they achieved in science, in art and in religion. The ruins of great buildings fill us with a desolation beyond the mere pity of the ruin of so beautiful a thing: they fill us with wonder whether there is any real progress ahead of us at all. We ask ourselves why we can go so far and no farther. At the very hour when I write we confront the possibility of another crash, another step back into what is rightly called a "dark age."

The most optimistic of us will admit that, supposing the setbacks are not so serious as they seem and that the stream of progress goes forward in spite of its backwaters, the pace might yet with advantage be quickened.

Where shall we look for a reasoned optimism? Let women come forward with something which is at least part of the answer.

It has often been pointed out that they have in their hands the first years of the life of children. How deep the impression made in these years may be is still a disputed point, but everyone knows that it is deep. Women have a vast responsibility here. It is certain

44

Women and the Next Civilization

that many of the discords in our nature begin while we are still too young to defend our own integrity. Some psychologists say that all our discords begin in the earliest years. The theory is not proved and, like other sweeping generalizations about human beings, is probably far too sweeping. No modification of it, however, will blind us to the fact that a great many injuries are traceable to the years of infancy.

And infancy is in the hands of women. What a responsibility! What an opportunity! Whatever responsibilities men may claim in later years they have never claimed either the right or the duty of looking after the infants of their race. That has always been in the hands of women.

The speed at which humanity might advance could be immeasurably quickened if women understood and accepted the position. The complexes, the repressions, the discords which so paralyse us could be indefinitely lessened. Our unbalanced characters, with their lopsided development, half childish, half mature, could be balanced and made sane. There *need* be no Peter Pans, no Mary Roses. It is difficult for us to imagine what life would be if we were as carefully, wisely and unselfishly handled on our entrance into maturity as we are, increasingly, handled on our entrance into life. No one who has attended the confinements of all sorts and kinds of women can fail to be struck with the courage and fortitude of almost all of them. What is needed now is that the same courage, the same selflessness and an even greater wisdom should be shown at the second birth.

In the world of the future there is no greater contribution to be made by any section of the community

45

than this; none which will add more to the strength and sanity of the rising generation. No one else can make it: it is in the hands of the mothers.

It has been seen that the power of women is very great, since they have been able to change humanity from a nomad to a settled race. This they did, and the doing was the beginning of civilization.

It is now time that they made a further contribution equally important. All that is lovely, all that is truly worthy to be called "mother-love" is needed. All that is unworthy, selfish and possessive has to be cast out. That is not asking too much of a passion so strong and so fundamentally noble. It will be repaid by the disappearance of the "filial ingratitude" of which mothers often complain, and of which the "ungrateful child" is unable to feel quite guiltless. Instead there will be created a new and more spiritual bond between mother and child. As I know no more dreadful feeling than that of a child who—and this is no exaggeration—*hates* his or her mother for making a claim on his very life which he cannot admit, so there is nothing lovelier than the passion of gratitude and the depth of understanding which I have found again and again in the hearts of children for parents who have made no selfish claims but have stood by and endured without resentment the awkward efforts of the young to stand on their own feet, make their own mistakes and live their own life.

Fathers have their responsibilities and powers too. We are beginning to realize this more and more. Probably we all know families whose life is darkened by paternal tyranny and in which it is the mother's difficult duty to keep the peace while guarding, as far

Women and the Next Civilization

as she can, the rightful liberties of her children. Yet this happens more rarely and is, bad as it is, less completely disastrous than a failure on the part of the mother.

It happens more rarely because fathers are not praised for such tyranny or encouraged to believe that it is due to a specially fine brand of fatherly affection, of which he has a right to be proud and for which his children ought to be grateful. On the contrary, he is recognized as a very selfish parent, and his children rebel or run away with far less heart-searching and self-reproach than when they rebel against their mother.

And it is less disastrous because the father really has not the same *power* to destroy his children's well-being as the mother has. There is a time, it is true, when he bulks more largely in the family eye, especially with his sons. They begin to feel their masculinity and to resent even the suspicion of being tied to their mother's apron-strings. They want things that their mother cannot give and their father can. They want a knowledge of the world—the man's world—and feel that he alone in the family possesses it. Daughters too stand in a very special relationship to fathers, as beautiful as the special relationship that exists between mothers and sons. One often notices that, as one woman put it to me, "the things their father punished in John and Harry are regarded as marks of genius in Elizabeth!"

Nevertheless the mother's power to help and to hinder is and remains stronger than the father's. Firstly, because it is established in the earliest years of the child's life, and the experiences of infancy and childhood can never be obliterated. Secondly, because there is always the physical tie between them and the knowledge, realized or not realized, that their mother risked her own life to give them theirs. This knowledge, however much it is overlaid by the passing of years or the discovery that in many cases the risk to life is slight or negligible, deeply influences the relationship of mother and child. It makes the child's rebellion far more difficult and more destructive to its own self-respect. It was a father into whose mouth Shakespeare put that terrible cry:

> "Ingratitude, thou marble-hearted fiend,
> More monstrous when thou show'st thee in a child
> Than the sea-monster"

but it is to the mother that ingratitude seems most monstrous, and the ingrate can very hardly escape his own condemnation of himself.

It is therefore the mother whose responsibility is the greater. It is for women to make the path straight for the rising generation.

Chapter III

Home and State: Individual and Nation

PEOPLE who believe, as I do, that the work of women will always be chiefly in the home must not forget that the home is *in* the nation. In the old days, before we won the vote, one of the chief arguments against our having it was that the nation was the man's job and the home the woman's. This argument leaves out of account the fact that as the nation is made up of homes, so homes are in the nation. The idea that the interests of men and women were entirely different and never met is so fantastic that it is hard to believe that anyone ever argued in this way, but they did. One writer even reduced the whole thing to a parable in which men were represented by birds and women by mice;* as though they were not only of a different sex but of a different species.

It is not necessary to combat such imbecilities to-day, fortunately: but the idea of a cleavage between the interests of men and women influences our minds even when they have rejected it. The consequence is that women have not done all they could—and will some day—in the service of the State. They have not realized that it is not enough to make one great and beneficent change, however great and however beneficent, in the history of the human race, but that change must go on.

Every thing that lives changes. It is a condition of

* Or the other way about. I don't remember which, and it does not matter.

Women's Partnership in the New World

life, and women ought to have grasped this first of all since they had the growing children in their hands. Instead, just as too many mothers have wanted their children to *stay* children, so they have wanted, or at least been content to see, the civilization they brought into being stand still.

It cannot. It grows, or it decays. It has been breaking down on an enormous scale in Europe during this century. And breaking down is a ruinous and horribly painful business. Can we in this country avoid it? Can we show the world how to avoid it in the future?

If there were men and women at the head of the State who knew that civilization must neither be pulled up by the roots nor left to rot where it stands, we should be able to combine stability and progress. Only when we do so can we really progress at all. The diehard whose pride it is to be for ever doing his hard dying in the last ditch is no greater an enemy to progress than the revolutionary whose eyes gleam at the thought of a terrific catastrophe and streets running with blood. Violent revolutions provoke violent reactions. The most crusted reactionary has to move a little bit with the times, and the reddest revolution brings some advance that cannot be cancelled; but between them they have made progress as difficult and as agonizing as it well can be. Let us begin to do better. Women must no longer pride themselves on their indifference to affairs of State.

Canvassing in a crowded London area for some reform, a visitor had difficulty in getting any answer to a knock at the door. At last it opened about six inches; a small section of a woman's face was seen;

Home and State: Individual and Nation

and a voice said, "Please go away. We aren't interested in anything here."

Of course there are men who are also not interested. Few of them think this indifference a positive virtue, though they may not be as ashamed of it as they should be. Lots of women actually pride themselves on it. But not to care enough to press forward is to make oneself a dead weight on those who do: and to make progress impossible or difficult is to provoke catastrophe.

It is a strange thing that again and again the pioneers of one generation become the immovable obstacles of the next. Or perhaps it is not really strange. The pioneer has had such a struggle that he is exhausted. He wants to sit down. That is no matter; but he wants everyone else to sit down too—even those who have not yet run a mile and have only just found out what fun it is to run. Besides (he thinks), have we not, largely through his efforts, run to the right place? We therefore not only *can* sit down, but we *ought* to sit down. There is no sense in going further. If we do, we may run over a precipice.

So he sits down and rests his old bones, probably with his back to the view. And the young ones, who are all for stretching their legs, hang around waiting for a lead from this great pioneer, until at last they go away and leave him—or run right over him in a rage.

Is this why women who built the home and led the human race into it want to sit down and stay there? It took an age—it took many ages—to build that home. Why leave it? Have we not done enough?

No, not enough.

Women's Partnership in the New World

"Build thee more stately mansions, O my soul,
  As the swift seasons roll!
  Leave thy low-vaulted past!
  Let each new temple, nobler than the last,
  Shut thee from heaven with a dome more vast,
  Till thou at length art free,
  Leaving thine outgrown shell by life's unresting sea!"*

That freedom is a long way off, but we must expect and work for it. If we change the metaphor and think of ourselves as builders rather than runners, we must build more and more nobly and more spaciously. The home must not be a prison but a palace. To achieve this we must begin to have the courage of our convictions, and this for women is not easy.

Women know that the home they have built is good. Of the outside world they know less. When men tell women that what is "all very well" in the home will "never do" outside it, they are apt to believe what they are told. "Outside" is the men's job, and they know best what to do about it. It is true they do not seem to have made a very good job of it up to now, but women will not improve matters by pushing in with ideas learned on the small scale that home life allows.

This is a profound mistake. The teaching of science should have taught us that long ago. Unfortunately, science is rather at a discount now, since its advance has taught people to make poison gas, bombing aeroplanes and high explosives, rather than more food, better houses and plenty for all. If women had applied themselves to the use of science in the home, the world might have done better, and it is not the fault of science that it

* Oliver W. Holmes.

has not. Let us make one application of its teaching now.

If a "law of nature" is true on a small scale, it will be true on a large scale also. The "law" of gravitation does not apply only to the china we drop (and break); it applies also to the stars. The "law" by which water "finds its own level" applies not only to the bathroom tap but to Niagara and to the sea.

The law of love which turns a house into a home will turn a world into a home too, when we muster up courage enough to try it.

It is true of the houses we live in. A house in which there is no love may be a hotel or a boarding-house or a block of self-contained flats; or it may be a prison, a fort or a lunatic asylum. It will not be a home. A home can only be created where there are human beings who love one another. Only so can they be "at home." The phrase is revealing. One can even "feel at home" in someone else's house if one is loved and welcomed. Studdert Kennedy has given us the heart of the matter: "When we are with a friend or someone we love deeply we are quite satisfied, and we no longer ask why we live or why we were born—we feel we were born for this."

Is there anyone who does not realize the truth of this? There are hours in the life of all thinking, feeling beings when they ask why they live or why they are born. It is not by any means always when we are suffering most from some calamity: it is when we feel that there is no purpose in life, and so no purpose in living. Life is hard. If we are to judge by the parable of the talents, it must be accepted that it is and will be hard.* But we should need no such parable if we

* "Thou knewest that I was an austere man."—Luke xix. 22.

53

would only face the facts for themselves. Life is a hard master and living a hard duty. Inevitably we ask ourselves the question: Is it worth while? But we no longer ask it "when we are with someone we love deeply." Love is itself an object and a purpose. To serve those we love deeply is a reason for living which we do not question. It makes the hard yoke of life an easy one and its burden no burden but a joy.*

This is why a mother likes to "do everything" for her child and would laugh at the idea that any service is too menial. Since love is her motive, all services are alike to her and all worth doing. If you ask her why she should sit up at night with a sick child or sacrifice her sleep to its comfort, she will hardly know how to answer you. There is no "why" in her mind; there is no question. When you love someone and that someone is in need, you do not ask why you were born. The reason is obvious.

If such sincere, unselfish love rules in the whole household, there is the solution to most of its problems. Those that are not solved can be cheerfully borne. Why? Because these people love one another! That is the only and sufficient answer. And most of the problems *are* solved because there is the will to solve them. Besides, love is so full of sympathy that it creates understanding. Where there is understanding we need not stand on our rights: we are more interested in the rights of the others. Justice gives way to love, for it is seen that mere human justice is not enough to create happy human relationships. It is

* "Take my yoke upon you and learn of me . . . and ye shall find rest for your souls. For my yoke is easy and my burden is light."—Matthew xi. 29 and 30.

Home and State: Individual and Nation

only love that can do that, and love is the divine justice.

It is useless to say that every member of the family must have (for example) the same food. One must have more, one less according to his needs. One must have meat, another milk. It is not selfishness or injustice which insists that the wage-earning father of a young family or the expectant mother must have special rights: it is wisdom. No reasonable person would question it. It takes, however, much more care and skill to decide all these things and to provide for them than is needed for the bare "justice" of a barrack or a prison, whose object is simply to deal out the same portion to each person! That requires very little thought, and the result is generally as unpleasing as the thought is small. For much the same reason most people dislike or very quickly tire of hotel food. It may be cooked by a highly skilled cook, and it will certainly command a much wider range of material; but it is not *individual*, and it cannot be. The food served in a good home may be much less varied, but it is much more carefully adapted to needs and tastes.

All this trouble is taken in the service of people we love. The result is nearly perfect—as nearly perfect as love can make it.

When, however, taught by their own experience women look abroad and challenge the standards of the world, they are told that their experience is of no value there—it is on too small a scale for the affairs of the nation. Probably the late Lord Birkenhead would have agreed that a home can and should be run on principles as nearly Christlike as human beings can achieve, but when it came to Ireland—

Women's Partnership in the New World

"you can't govern Ireland by the Sermon on the Mount!"*

Why not? If it works on the small scale, why not on the large? Science itself gives us the answer; and every scientist knows that the great powers that we use to do the vast tasks of industry have to be tried out first on the small scale of the laboratory and the workshop —or even the home. Is it a mere coincidence that shows us James Watt studying the steam that rose from his mother's kettle, and learning from that the use of the great steam-engine that changed the face of the world?

Proofs that the friendly atmosphere of the home is the one in which international affairs could flourish are not lacking. Lord Birkenhead s conciliatory attitude changed Southern Ireland from a bitter enemy to at least a fairly friendly neutral. Does anyone in his senses doubt that a continuation of the Black-and-Tan policy would have thrown Eire into Hitler's arms? But there are greater examples than this; examples in which the good-will was far stronger and the results far more successful.

The most wonderful of all perhaps is the case of Canada and the United States. Here is a frontier of five thousand miles, undefended by a single fortress, gun or soldier. No one on either side of the frontier asks for defences. The suggestion that they could ever be necessary would be regarded as a joke, and rather a silly one at that. Unfortunately, the sheer success of

* To his credit, however, let it be pointed out that it was when Lord Birkenhead gave up the methods of the Black and Tans and, by a friendly approach to the Irish leaders, brought himself and them a little nearer to the Sermon on the Mount, that he arrived at something like a solution.

Home and State: Individual and Nation

the method by which the peace is kept is such that people take it for granted and never stop to ask to what it is due. It is like the good home in that. No one asks why there are so many and such good ones: they are taken for granted. And so is the peace between the United States of America and Canada.

But it was not always so. There was at one time bitter enmity between the two countries, and there were— and still are—many matters on which questions leading to wars might arise. It is a pity that so few English people know the history of the Canadian frontier, for it would be an inspiration to them to-day if they did.

Here is a brief summary.

Matters connected with the frontiers of Canada and the United States are in the hands of a Commission of six; three Americans and three Canadians. These commissioners, however, are sworn to regard themselves as impartial servants of the good of both countries, and not as representatives either of Canada or of the United States, sent there to press the point of view of their own countries. They are there to consider every question that comes up with a view to finding the best solution—the *best*, and not merely the best for one country or another.* The fact that each nation

* "These six commissioners, half American and half Canadian, are pledged to a viewpoint that is American in the *continental* sense. They must regard the people on both sides of the boundary as equally entitled to their best possible judgment. There can be no smartness nor jockeying in such an organization. All six commissioners represent the same broad international constituency." See *The Conquest of a Continent*, by Osborne and Osborne. This story of the relationship between Canada and the United States is a most enlightening and encouraging book for present-day reading.

has three representatives on the Commission in spite of the fact that one has a population of about 10 millions and the other of 120 or 130 millions makes the arrangement even more striking. It is well said that "such a remarkable departure from the traditions of the past is, of course, only practicable in the case of two countries feeling for each other such mutual confidence and respect as exists between Canada and the United States."*

Readers will perhaps argue that the task of the commissioners has been an easy one, since there are no really difficult or important questions at issue between the two countries. This is a fantastic misconception. There was, first of all, the terrific business of fixing the frontier between Canada and the U.S.A. Anyone who knows the world at all knows how many. and how savage have been the wars arising from the delineation of frontiers. These wars are raging in all their ghastly destructiveness now. And when the question of the Canadian frontier had to be tackled, there were American, Canadian, British, French, Spanish and Red Indian interests to be considered, and considered in an ignorance of the geography of the continent to be divided which was only surpassed by ignorance of its natural resources.† And the commissioners approached their task from viewpoints so far apart as a claim from the American side to the

* *The Conquest of a Continent,* p. 91.

† "Neither side knew much about what it had and consequently could not frame an intelligent desire of what it wished to retain or possess. The most striking thing about the entire situation was a complete lack of basic, reliable information."—*The Conquest of a Continent,* p. 8.

Home and State: Individual and Nation

whole of what is now the Dominion of Canada—and, on the British side, to all that is now the United States of America except a narrow strip of land on the Atlantic coast!

Yet, in spite of all, peace was kept. In spite of all, each problem has been faced and solved. The story of it covers a period of over a hundred years. The work of the commissioners continues to the present day, though the frontier itself was finally settled in 1910. Again and again matters of the utmost difficulty had to be handled, and again and again, especially at first, it seemed as if the whole arrangement must break down and guns, forts, ships of war and armies be substituted for arguments and conciliation. "Before the war of 1812 and while it was being waged citadel and arsenal came into being. Naval yards were set up and armed craft appeared on the waters of the St. Lawrence and the Great Lakes. Hostile forts frowned at each other from opposite shores. An armament race had begun; and had it been permitted to continue, we would have been looking back on years of suspicion, enmity and hatred, instead of rejoicing in a century of peace. In the course of the war of 1812, as many as twenty armed vessels were constructed in the naval yards at Kingston, Ontario. One of these, the *St. Lawrence*, was actually larger in size, and carried more guns, than Nelson's frigate *Victory* at the Battle of *Trafalgar*. Within three years of the conclusion of the war, however, we had determined to place our reliance upon reason instead of upon force, and to substitute for any surviving ill-will such a measure of solid goodwill as should bridge succeeding years."*

* *The Conquest of a Continent*, pp. 83 and 84.

Women's Partnership in the New World

In spite of all difficulties, the breaking-point was never reached. Reason prevailed. The peace was kept; kept so perfectly that my readers are wondering why I make such a pother about the whole matter.

But if they would read for themselves they would not wonder. Instead they would ask themselves what was the secret of such an amazing victory of reason over passion and of common sense over national pride, greed and stupidity.

The secret is here. "We had determined to . . . substitute for any surviving ill-will such a measure of solid goodwill as to bridge succeeding years."

Solid goodwill! Here is the heart of the matter. The difficulties were mountainous. Many of them must have seemed at times insurmountable. But all were surmounted, because there was present "a solid goodwill."

"Aristide Briand, late Premier and Foreign Minister of France, on more than one occasion expressed the desire and hope that a similar commission might be created to deal with questions along the frontiers between France and Germany. At the meeting of the Institute of Pacific Relations in Shanghai one of the delegates spoke of the Commission as an example of what might be accomplished between Japan and Soviet Russia in dealing with the vexed problem of the boundary between Siberia and Manchuquo."* What is this but to say that the principle that runs a home and makes it a good home is the principle on which the world can be run and without which it is a frightful world? The frontier between France and Germany is short indeed compared with that between Canada and

* *The Conquest of a Continent*, p. 110.

Home and State: Individual and Nation

the United States. Every mile of it is known to the geographer, every area of fertile or unfertile land, every mine, every source of wealth, can be measured and valued: yet war succeeds war along that tragic frontier because there is no solid goodwill to settle it.

To create goodwill seems to be no one's business. Why should it be? In the world of international politics it is every nation for itself, and the devil take the hindmost. "You can't govern Europe by the Sermon on the Mount." By what then can you govern it? By suspicion, enmity and violence? Yes—if you like. But do you like? Is this tragedy what anyone likes?

The nations after all are only people—only men and women and children like all of us. What is true of us in our own land and in our own homes is still true when we call ourselves "the Nations" or "the Powers." We want to feel that our rulers are doing their best for all of us, but we know—or we should know—that none of us can be quite happy and at peace while one is sullen and discontented. One malcontent can cast a gloom over a whole household. It is incredible what harm he can do. Merely to resent his resentment is waste of time, however. We must cure him if we can, even if it means stretching a point beyond sheer "justice." I write "justice" in inverted commas, for who knows what justice is? It has been rightly said that if we are to trace every wrong back to the first wrong-doer, we should have to go back to Cain. If we go back to Cain, we shall never get to the beginning at all and our time is wasted.

What mother, hearing an uproar among her children and going to see what is wrong, has not been met with the cry "he began it!" raised by every child in the turmoil? And who is so foolish as to insist on finding out "who began it" instead of quieting the noise by a judicious mixture of firmness and affection, which convinces by its "solid goodwill"? Generally it is quite useless to try to trace the quarrel to its beginning, though it is good ultimately to try because the effort shows a desire to be fair. But all the time one knows that the "beginning" is far deeper down and further back than we suppose, and most of the children, if not all, have had a share in it. It is more possible and more important to find the cause than the criminal.

Who indeed is the criminal? One child perhaps stands out. He is always a trouble-maker, he is a constant factor in every row. He then is the cause of it? But what is the cause of him? His health? His temperament? These he has in part inherited, in part owes to circumstances. His inheritance is from you O mother, from you O father! Then you too are on the defensive. You too had parents, bad parents perhaps, ancestors from whom you in your turn inherited the difficulties that make your difficult child. And if his circumstances have been wrong, is that his fault? Or yours? Or the fault of the social system of which you and he are a part? Was he too poor or too rich, or uneducated or educated wrongly? The house in which he lives, is it too small, too crowded or insanitary? His school, did that not fit him? Were the classes too large? Were the teachers at fault? And, if so, whose fault was their fault? Once more we begin the wearisome round of child and man, parent and offspring, the social system and all the rest of it. *All* are in default, and we who began with a scrap in the nursery find ourselves questioning the universe.

62

Home and State: Individual and Nation

Of course the more we know of human nature and all its circumstances the better; but the more we know the more we realize that "if we want to find who began" the trouble we must "go back to Cain."

Once more what is true in the nursery holds good through life.

To read the history of one continent alone—Europe —is to learn this lesson. Trace the course of one question only, and we shall find that it goes back to Cain. Germany and France have a frontier. For generations now they have fought over it. First one, then the other, is on top. That one takes more than he should. The other bides his time. This is what we call peace! He sees his time has come and seizes his opportunity. This is war! If we ask whose fault it is, we find ourselves back in the nursery and we hear the old cry—"he began it"!

There is not a nation which "began" any trouble but has its real or fancied reason for redress. If then you jump at the word "fancied" and declare that that is the root of the matter, for some nations are naturally bad and will *fancy* a grievance that they have not got and go to war about it, I put it to you that a *fancied* reason shows something as harmful as a real one, and more so, just because it is disguised and so unrecognized. It was a wise physician who said, "If a man thinks he is ill when he is not, he is very ill indeed."* Is that not wisdom?

A child says he has a headache or a stomachache and is unable to go to school. On being told that he need not go he rapidly recovers. It is not enough to say that in that case there was nothing the matter with

* Dr. Schofield, *The Mental Factor in Medicine.*

63

him. There was. There is. It is not a headache, but it is something, and probably something rather more complicated than a headache. Perhaps he is punished for malingering, but the fact that he is punished shows that his parents or guardians are quite sure that there is something wrong, else why punish him? The proposed cure may be as useless as an aspirin for a non-existent headache, but it *is* a proposed cure, and why cure if there is nothing wrong? A more enlightened method would probably be to find out if there is any special reason for the child's unwillingness to go to school and, whether the answer is that he has not done his homework or that he is bullied at school or something quite different, but the fact that we put the question shows our recognition of "something wrong."

Most parents take a good deal of trouble nowadays to find the answers to such questions as these, and the result is, we hope and believe, that our children will grow up with fewer "repressions" and "complexes" than we did. We take this trouble because we are concerned not only with the child's past—which we cannot now alter—but with its present happiness and future well-being. In fact, we care enough for these things to go very carefully and think hard before we decide how to handle a trouble of this kind.

"My little girl is always ill when it is time to start for Sunday school," said a mother. "She isn't really ill at all. What can I do?" "Are you absolutely certain she isn't ill?" says the psychologist consulted. "Yes, because she, being naturally a simple soul and not at all a good liar, recovers the moment I say she needn't go." "Then you had better insist on her going, but explain to her that you know she thinks she feels badly

Home and State: Individual and Nation

(for she almost certainly thinks she does) and are not angry or disgusted with her. You yourself, you may assure her, have often felt ill at the thought of doing something you don't want to do; but it is really better to do the thing all the same, or one may grow into the sort of person who can never be counted on, or count on herself, to be brave at a crisis. All children want to be brave, and will therefore generally respond to the appeal and, doing so, preserve and increase their own self-respect. To be merely rebuked for a liar would destroy it and set a barrier between the rebuker and the child. On the other hand, to act as though you believed in her headache when you did not raises another kind of barrier, no less disastrous, and is liable to turn her into the sort of woman who, in after life, will bully her husband into yielding to every unreason-able demand for fear she will burst into tears or have a sick headache if he does not."

This is a simple instance, and there are many far more subtle, and many for which all our love and care fail to find the right way; but I use it just because it is simple and very common, being within the experience of most of us, both as the childish malingerer and the grown-up guardian. It is so clear that a fancied grievance and a fancied pain alike show that something is wrong, just as wrong as and often more disastrous than a "real" suffering. The suffering *is* real, even though the cause may be misunderstood.

Contrast the loving care with which the modern mother tries to find the cause of suffering with the rough-and-ready methods of international politics. If a nation is a trouble-maker, it is set down as one who loves to make trouble. In fact, it is "bad" and must be punished. Every effort is made to prove that the wrongs it complains of are not wrongs and that its grievances are quite imaginary. If we should follow the family plan, our first effort would not be to prove that there was no real grievance but to find out whether there was any reality in it. The psychologist first asked the mother of the malingering child whether she was absolutely *sure* that the headache was not a real headache before going a step further. If, however, it was proved that the headache was not "a real headache," that did not prove that the sense of suffering was not real. The next question must be why the child says it has a headache when it has not. That needs a lot more patience, but no wise mother would fail to ask it, and no wise mother would be quite satisfied until she had found the answer. If she does so, she can then deal with the "real" cause of a perfectly "real" complaint.

Moreover, she will know well that children are so different that what causes acute suffering in one leaves another untouched. This, which was always known to the common-sensible, has now been accepted even by the clever. A difficult child who is growing up to be a nuisance to the whole family is known to have suffered some rebuff or punishment when a mere infant, which deeply wounded its self-respect, and the wound, festering, has poisoned its life. But another child in the same family has been treated in the same way and suffered no injury at all. Every time the question of flogging in schools comes up for discussion, men write to the newspapers to say either that they were flogged and so deeply injured by the indignity that they never got over it; or that they were flogged more than once and never troubled their heads about

Home and State: Individual and Nation

it again. Some will declare that they can never be grateful enough for the pains taken by their elders to explain the nature of any offence committed by them, and so substitute a moral self-condemnation for the condemnation of physical chastisement inflicted by someone else; while others as determinedly affirm that they would infinitely have preferred a thrashing and release from the "pi-jaw."* We, no doubt, all have our preferences both in punishment and in the people who like one kind better than the other; the extravert who would rather be punished from without, or the intravert who prefers to judge himself. The point is not what we like best in our children but what is the right thing for each child. It is unpardonable in us to "treat them all alike," for they are not all alike and what suits one will destroy another.

Nations are as different as the people who make up the nations. Unfortunately, there are no nations that will play the part of mothers! But should we not try? Of course we like some better than others. How should we not? Sometimes they are the nations most like ourselves; quite as often they are those that are different. In either case the point is not whether we do or do not like them, but how we and they can so act towards one another as to make a happy relationship possible. It is only another way of saying, a happy world.

---

* A popular and highly respected magistrate of a great city could not refrain from delivering a short lecture to those whom he was about to sentence, especially if they were of the working class, as he was. On one occasion the victim, a personal friend, found it intolerable. "Oh, come off it, Charlie," was his cry: "double the sentence and let me off the sermon."

Women's Partnership in the New World

An instance only too tragically familiar to us is what is called the "war-guilt clause" in the Treaty of Versailles. When it was discussed, some of its defenders argued that, because it can be understood in some rather cryptic and non-natural sense, the Germans "ought not" to resent it. The point, however, is not whether they *ought* to resent it but whether they *do*; just as the point in a family quarrel is not whether a child *ought* to be permanently injured in spirit by a flogging but whether it *is*. Some people prefer the sort of temperament that takes a flogging without resentment and thinks no more about it: others believe that the finer temperament is the one most deeply wounded by such treatment. What is that to the purpose? *How* people feel—and how nations feel—is the point; and not whether we like their feeling.

These things sound elementary enough when put down, yet how continually we flout them! There are "Institutes of Child Psychology" and "Child Guidance" clinics, but the work of the Institute of International Psychology has hardly begun its researches and has excited little interest. Mothers have begun to realize the importance of such knowledge of their children, and for this we may thank them. I was present at a lecture given by a distinguished psychologist on the training of children, which was largely attended by an audience of mothers. They sat listening with strained attention, in an agony of suspense lest they should learn that they had already, by some indiscretion, injured the souls of their children. The questions put to the speaker after the lecture showed the intensity of the interest felt by all and their eagerness to learn.

Can anyone imagine a Peace Conference preceded

Home and State: Individual and Nation

by a lecture to the delegates on the psychology of the
nations concerned? Would delegates attend such a
lecture? Why should they? Their object is not to do
the best they can for one another but the best they can
for themselves. They consider each other's feelings only
so far as those feelings can be made useful to themselves.
If anyone had argued at Versailles that the war-guilt
clause would have a disastrous psychological effect on
the German people, making their recovery infinitely
difficult and creating an almost incurable lesion in
their souls, he would have been derided. Who cared
what the psychological effect on Germany might be?
A delegate might have had the courage to say that it
was not true that Germany *alone* was guilty of the war,
and he might conceivably have been heard. At least
he would not have been thought to be discussing a
matter that was wholly beside the mark. To raise the
question of the psychology of Germany, or indeed of
any other nation, would have been thought idiotic.

And yet, if we strip the matter of such words as
psychological and *neurosis* and the like, we must know
that as we can never have peace in our homes while
one member of the family, rightly *or wrongly*, feels
deeply injured by the rest, so we can never have peace
in the world while one nation feels like this. What do
we really want? The fun of hurting each other's feelings?
Or peace?

At a meeting during the election following the last
war I heard a masterly speech on the subject of the
terms of peace. The speaker, though not nominally a
Christian, analysed the situation in a way that showed
we could not hurt the Germans in any way whatever
without hurting ourselves. It was a magnificent sermon

on the text: "If one member suffers, all the members share its suffering; if one member is honoured, all the members share its honour."* The audience, drunk with the sufferings and the victories of war, was uproariously hostile at first. At last they ceased to be uproarious, silenced by the crushing weight of the speaker's logic. *They did not cease to be hostile.* At the close a woman rose and said, "We don't care if we do hurt ourselves, so long as we hurt Germany"—a remark which was greeted with yells of delight.

To this there could of course be no answer. But if we once realize the impossibility of hurting each other without hurting ourselves, we have gone quite a long way and shall at last even stop *wanting* to hurt each other.

Even so we shall still have a long way to go. We must learn not only that we cannot hurt any member of the family without producing an atmosphere in which no one can be happy, but that we cannot *ignore* the suffering of anyone without being the poorer for it. It has been truly said that the cruellest of men could not sit comfortably at his feast if he must eat it in the presence of starving men, women and children. It is only because we need not do so that we can gorge ourselves in peace. Those who have carried their service into famine-stricken places have recorded the dreadful difficulty of eating—without gorging!—while those they come to serve are still far below the poverty line. In order to carry on their work of mercy they must eat and eat enough, even if barely enough. On their ability to keep going depends the whole administration of relief, and their lives are as necessary to all as the life

* 1 Corinthians xii. 26. Moffatt's translation.

Home and State: Individual and Nation

of the breadwinner in a poor home which depends on him for maintenance. But it is a hard necessity, made almost intolerable by the sight of starving people all around. It is comparatively easy when they are not "all around," but at least far enough off to be out of sight.

We must somehow develop a greater sensitiveness towards those whom we do not see.

We have already learned how to hear the human voice carried by the amplifier across the largest hall, by the telephone across land and ocean, by the microphone round the world. We can see with the help of the telescope across the myriad miles of space and count millions of stars where our forefathers saw only thousands; and with the help of the microscope things to them invisible. With the use of the intellect we can count and measure where no instrument can give us sight—atoms, nuclei, electrons. Can we spiritually advance to such a height as this? Can we see with the eyes of the mind and heart the sufferings of human beings in China and hear the cries of the prisoners in a concentration camp? If we can do so, we shall no longer be able to ignore them, and we shall know then that it is as dangerous to do so as to ignore the microbe in our blood. That we did not know that we had been infected with malaria by the bite of a mosquito one summer evening will not save us from malaria. We "ignored" it in the literal sense, meaning that we were ignorant of it; but we suffer the consequences of our ignorance all the same. It will be remembered that Christ did not accuse the man who built his house upon the sand of wickedness but of folly.* He "shall be

* Matthew vii. 26 and 27.

likened unto a foolish man," and his house will fall
and "great will be the fall of it."

So the sufferings of one unhappy nation can infect
the world with pain, and the sufferings of one part of
any nation, though the more fortunate draw away from
them and escape the sight of their suffering, infect us all.

The mothers of the world know this best and feel it
most deeply. A naughty child may be banished from
the room, and the rest of the family forget him. She
cannot. Her day is spoilt. She will steal away from the
riotous party and go upstairs to listen at the door to
hear whether her child is crying, or sulking, or ready
to be restored to the family circle. Without it that circle
is incomplete, and nothing is as it should be. If one
child suffer, its mother at least must suffer with it. She
cannot forget it merely because she has been forced to
send it out of her sight.

We must go further. We must take action to bring
back into the heart of things the one who suffers and
is outcast. With babies how instinctively one does it!
If a baby cries, we try by all means to distract its
attention and to offer it something that will please it.
If a child is unhappy, we are troubled and seek the
cause. It is not only because its cries or its sulks spoil
our pleasure: it is because we really need its happiness
and because it can *give* us something. In a family
everyone has something to give to the rest. The relationship of parents to children is a lovely one, but the
relationship of each parent to each child has its peculiar
value. A mother will perhaps give her deepest love to
her son, a father to his daughters. The eldest, the
youngest, the ugly duckling, the physically weak—all
have their own appeal to parents and to one another,

Home and State: Individual and Nation

and because of this they have something to give without which the others would be the poorer. The devoted love and care lavished not only by mothers but by the teachers in "special schools" on children of defective intelligence is one of the loveliest things on earth. It is divine in its selfless beauty. Human nature never shines more radiantly than in such places.

But if this is so, who will deny that the defective child has also given something to us? We hope some day for a world in which there will be no such sufferers: but while they are here they teach us love and pity, which wisely used will at last take away their pain.

I have watched the nurse of a defective child hanging over it with absorbed devotion, trying to win from it some response to some appeal, rejoicing when response is apparent with a delight which, weighed in the balance of cold worldly wisdom, would seem fantastically out of proportion to its cause. Did she gain nothing from him? Was the world no richer for that amazing love? No one can say so.

If the value we find in one another in our personal lives is so great, even when, as in the case of the "deficient" child, it would seem utterly negligible to those who have not experienced it, we may expect it to be great between nations also. And so it is.

Some nations seem to be more gifted than others. We read their history and are moved to gratitude for what they have given to the world. We rejoice that they had the opportunity to give; we lament their oppression and their downfall. The more we know of national histories the more we shall rejoice in one another. We can still study the philosophy, the religion and the art of China, the spiritual genius, the great

73

temples, the serene gigantic Buddhas of India and the East. We are further from the ancient Egyptians, but still we explore and dig and search for the records of that great civilization. Greece is a name of wonder for its amazing achievements in almost every department of life. Palestine has our deeper reverence, because its people gave us the Son of God. There is no end to the debts we willingly acknowledge to these "foreign" peoples. And where their history has been unwritten or forgotten we gaze on the relics still existing, wonder at their beauty and wish we could know more of the race that created them and the reason of its passing.

Why this passionate interest in the Pyramids or in Angkor Vat and this stupid contempt for the gifts that nations can give to each other to-day? Perhaps, had we known them, we should not have "liked" the ancient builders of these wonders of the world. We might have fought them, defeated them, wiped them out. Someone apparently did so in the end. How many times were people defeated and wiped out *before* they gave their gifts to the world? We shall never know. If we consider that vast peoples such as those of India and China gave no greater gifts than tiny ones like Palestine and Greece, we shall begin to realize what ignorance and oppression has robbed us of.

There is no member of the great family of nations which has not something to give, as there is no member of the little families we live in which cannot contribute something. If it is not allowed to do so it suffers; and we suffer. We shall never know how much we have lost. We shall never know what the child we lost might have been or done in the world. We shall never know, though perhaps we may dimly guess, what heights

74

Home and State: Individual and Nation

might have been reached by the misunderstood, mishandled child if he had been better understood, more carefully handled. We begin to guess, but our very guessing brings home to us our ignorance and leaves us wondering what we and the world have lost.

I am sure it was not a woman who was first guilty of that idiotic saying that "if a man is a genius nothing can prevent his coming to the top." Women know too well that it depends on the *kind* of genius. Some great men and women are equipped with great moral and physical strength and fight their way up and out with a hearty enjoyment of the struggle. Others, differently made, are crushed in the process, not because they had not genius, and not necessarily because they were of inferior mettle; but because the odds were heavier still or they of a different temperament. If a child is blind from birth because of the sins of its ancestors, its inborn genius for painting will not be so much as guessed at. If its body is infected with disease, it may die as young as Keats died, but that does not prove that it had no genius. So a man or woman may, by bad luck, have a sensitiveness to just those circumstances which may be theirs and may be overwhelmed by them. This does not prove that they had no genius.

Of all the "easy speeches that comfort cruel men" this one seems to me the worst. It is so ignorant, so smug, so cruel. How do we know that all the men and women who really had it in them to serve the world greatly "came out on top"? We do not know. We cannot even dimly guess. We might as well say that a man of genius can never be blown to bits by a bomb in war as that he can never be crushed out of shape or out of life by circumstances in the battle of life. And

75

the sensitive and delicate temperament is as valuable a part of human life as the ebullient and generous-hearted extravert.

So it is with the nations. Some of the small or weak nations can be so bludgeoned and oppressed that they produce little or nothing. It is all they can do to keep their foothold in the world, and sometimes more than they can do. Maybe they fail to do it. Can anyone think of them, I do not say without pity, but without a haunting sense of loss? What might they not have given us had they been free?

One of the outstanding features of the League of Nations at its best was the chance it gave to the smaller nations to give their gifts to the world. In those early years the names that come to our memory are not only those of Cecil, Briand, Viviani and Stresemann—representatives of the Great Powers—but of Nansen, Hymans, Branting and Motta, who came from the little nations of Norway, Sweden, Belgium and Switzerland. Madariaga of Spain and Politis of Greece and Wellington Koo of China served the League also, and through it the world. Probably none of these would have been heard of outside their own countries but for the great Society of Nations. It was the nearest thing the world has yet conceived to a *family* of nations. Its failure must not leave us forgetful of its great qualities, and this was one of them—this opportunity of service to the whole world, through their finest men, of the little nations.

What is true among the nations is true of the classes also. What could be more senseless than the belief that men and women of genius "always come to the top" in face of the enormous difficulties that cramp the

76

Home and State: Individual and Nation

children of one class as compared with those of another? How do we *know* that they all "come to the top"— those whose gifts might have taken them there in other circumstances? When they die we must admit it! As with Keats, death may cut short the life of genius even before it has fully flowered. But the death which would not have overtaken more fortunate children is not the only way by which genius or talent is frustrated.

A child, sent out into the street by its mother, struggling through the pains of another confinement, may be run over and killed. It might, we shall all agree, have been a genius. But another on whom came all too early the burden of contributing something to the family income may have been frustrated without dying. We say he would not have been overwhelmed if he had truly been a genius? He may retort that if he had been more selfish and unscrupulous, he would have climbed to the top over the bodies of his brothers and sisters. Are we sure he is in the wrong, and not we?

There are of course people whose gifts, character and circumstances are so harmonious that they can climb upward without treading on other people, but it is not always so. Sometimes, when one hears it said with a sneer that the poor are the hardest masters and women the most exacting when placed in positions of authority, one wonders whether this is not due to the fact that they had to be ruthless in their ambition before they could force their way up. If they could not persuade themselves to be ruthless, they must stay where they are; and if that happens to be on the bottom rung, are we to say they have not the resolution or the courage to rise higher? Or that they are too compassionate and too loyal?

77

Women's Partnership in the New World

All this should teach us how to value the genius of the small and weak nations as we are learning to value that of the individual. But how slow we are! If a nation, oppressed and weak, does not show the world what it can do, we think contemptuously that it can do nothing. If, under the heel of the oppressor, its people develop the defects of the cramped and persecuted, we make that an excuse for leaving them unhelped.

Mothers do not so with their children.

Chapter IV

What Next?

To women belongs the credit of beginning the first civilization. They converted humanity from the wandering to the settled life. In that settled life they did the work of the artist, the craftsman and the worker in the fields.

This showed, as I have said, both that their power is very great and that it was used in obedience to the truest instincts of human nature. In the home was born all those things which make us human or, as we now say, civilized.

But what is it to be "civilized"? One is tempted more and more to put the word in inverted commas. Else the critic in us immediately wakes and asks: "What do you mean by 'civilization'?" Is this mad world in which men live to-day "civilization"? Is it not more like savagery? Or perhaps a lunatic asylum? And the critic's words strike home, for indeed much that we see is worse than barbarism; it is insanity.

Something has gone wrong. Let us examine the great civilizations of the past. We observe that they have one thing in common: they all came to an end.

I think when those great civilizations arose men believed that they would stand for ever or, if not stand, go forward and upward by an almost automatic process. I think the optimism of our forefathers in the Victorian Age was not due to the fact that Darwin had written a great book on evolution. Not at all. It was due to the fact that men were prosperous, well fed, on the top of the world. In this mood they read *The Origin of Species* and learned that it was natural to go from not-so-good to good, from good to better, and from better to best. This progress, it is true, must be a fight, called "the struggle for existence," but since it was also natural for men to fight, that was nothing to worry them. So, generally without reading it, men made *The Origin of Species* their Bible.

If they had read it, they might not have felt so sure of the future. If they had belonged to those classes whose lives are described in some of the novels of Dickens—chimney sweepers, charity schoolboys, "paupers"—they would also have felt less sure. But the men of whom I think did not belong to those classes. They were comfortable, prosperous and optimistic. It is really difficult not to be optimistic when you are comfortable.

It is equally difficult to remain optimistic when you are uncomfortable. It is not therefore reasonable for us to sneer at Victorian optimists because their optimism was not based on either intellectual conviction or religious faith but on the unreasoned and far from religious sense of being exceedingly comfortable, for we are doing the same thing now, only the other way round.

To-day, when we are more than uncomfortable—when we are tragically unhappy and unsafe—we see through that easy optimism and feel that we are wiser than our fathers.

Are we? Is our pessimism not the result of our suffering just as much as their optimism was the result of their prosperity?

I believe it is. I believe we should not be content to

What Next?

point out that there is no reason whatever for hope in the future of the race; that all civilizations have come to an end; that men have risen to great heights, and perhaps greater than we have reached, but have always crashed at last. We should not travel from India to China and from China to Egypt merely in order to encourage ourselves in our gloom.

We should travel indeed—if we are lucky enough to be able to travel—but in a better mood than this. We should perhaps even take for our motto:

"I see that all things come to an end; but thy commandments are exceeding broad."*

It may be that some of these commandments have been forgotten. Why not use our knowledge and our travels in order to look and see?

It may be that our pessimism is just as unreasonable and unreasoned as other men's optimism. We shall find perhaps that we think "all things come to an end" merely because our things are doing so and the process is painful. This is not flippancy but a serious comment on a very serious drift of opinion to-day. Many leaders of religious opinion are preaching a doctrine of despair. To do right, they say, is impossible. There is an original sinfulness in the nature of man that creates in him a perpetual discord. He *cannot* do the perfect thing. Not only his circumstances but himself makes it impossible. They quote with despairing energy the cry of St. Paul: "The good that I would I do not: but the evil that I would not that I do."† They seem to forget that the same great man wrote that we should "all come in the unity of the faith and of the knowledge of

* Psalm cxix. 96.   † Romans vii. 19.

the Son of God, unto a perfect Man, unto the measure of the stature of the fullness of Christ."* And that a yet greater Teacher called us to be "perfect as our Father which is in heaven is perfect."†

It is a futile business to throw texts at one another, and there is much to be said on both sides of this ancient controversy. I speak of it here only to remind myself and my readers of the extent to which our moods reflect our thoughts. It is because we have made, after the high hopes and "optimism" of the nineteenth century, such a ghastly mess of the twentieth, that we are impressed with the gloomy fact of original sin. It is our grief and not our intelligence that rules our thoughts. We have nothing to boast over our fathers who were hopeful because they were happy: we others are pessimists because we are sad.

Let us bear this in mind, and, without waiting to solve a problem as old as human thought, look at this business of civilization with eyes as clear of prejudice as we can make them. What *is* civilization? Why do civilizations rise and fall? Can we perhaps avoid this tragedy ourselves? Shall we not at least try?

I do not doubt but that the fall of each civilization in turn has been differently caused, nor do I doubt but that in each case there have been several causes combined. Human nature is very complex. But to see *any* of the causes of decline is something. To see it may help to overcome the pessimism of an age of catastrophe, give us the power to see beyond the disaster, set us on the road upwards even before we have touched bottom.

Let us look at these fallen civilizations. They may teach us something more than pity.

* Ephesians iv. 13.   † Matthew v. 48.

What Next?

What remains of them for us to see? Chiefly, their art. The great temples of the Egyptians, their pyramids, their colossal statues, their ornaments, furniture, jewellery—these are still here for us to see and admire. We get some idea of the history of Egypt, its religion, its laws and its science, from these objects. It is they which make us refer to the period of Egypt's greatness as "a great civilization." So with China. We look at its lovely buildings, its marbles and tiles and gilding, and we see here also "a great civilization." India offers us the same wealth. The glory of Greece is of the same kind. We look at the Parthenon and, if there were nothing else to look at or to read, we should still accept the silent witness of this beauty to "a great civilization" of the Greeks. Some of the wonders of the world have disappeared, but even the record of them makes us speak with reverence of the ancient civilizations that produced them. We know that they were glorious, and so, we say, the people who gave them to the world were "civilized."

It is a good judgment. Who will challenge it? It is a much nobler judgment than that which assesses "a great power" by its armaments. The verdict of the world is more just than the passing idolatry of force. Not armies and arms but temples and works of art make a civilized nation.

But let us look a little closer. By whom were these works actually carried out? By a mass of slave labour. It is with a shock that we realize this. It must be faced, however. The labour of millions of slaves was needed to create the wonders of the world. The Great Wall of China, the Pyramids, the temples, were created by human toil so great as to be, to our modern ideas,

83

*in*human. The stones are cemented with blood and sweat.

Only a few years ago I saw in China the work being carried out for the erection of a vast tomb to the memory of Sun Yat Sen, the founder of the Chinese Republic. I was told that a magnificent road was being driven straight through the heart of the country and of the city of Nanking, along which the body of the hero would be carried to rest. That it might be straight, many houses had to be demolished. Such compensation as the State could afford was to be paid, but it was little, and in fact money does not compensate people for the loss of their homes. Many had committed suicide in their despair.

When I was in Nanking the road had reached the foot of the hill on the slopes of which the vast tomb was being built. A great staircase of stone was the work now in hand. It was already an imposing sight. I wish it may be possible for me some day to see the finished work, if indeed it has been finished. Of this I am not sure, for China has of late years been building herself a nation, which is a nobler memorial to the life of her great man than any tomb can be. Even as it was, however, unfinished and bare, I am glad to have seen it. It is a great sight.

But I cannot forget the inhuman toil that was being given to its building. There was no machinery; there were no cranes, no trucks, no engines. An enormous number of human beings carried on their shoulders the huge weights of stone and other material up the hill to their place. I saw a few—a very few—strings of donkeys on the hillside. I saw on the road below men pushing wheelbarrows full of stones. Apart from these

What Next?

—and to push such a wheelbarrow is itself a weary labour—there was nothing; nothing but human arms and backs and shoulders, nothing but human flesh and blood and muscle, to raise that vast stairway up the hillside and crown it with that glorious tomb.

From a little distance it looked like an enormous anthill. But these were not ants; they were men.

How was the Great Wall built? How the great works of Egypt and Rome? The pictures, carvings, hieroglyphics tell us. They were built by incredible numbers of human beings—slaves. Pharaoh, we know, used the people of Israel as his labourers. He was not the first or the only slave-driver. Every great work of building in the past was built in the same way.

Nor is this all. It was the existence of this mass of slavery that made the culture we have agreed to call "civilization" *possible*. It is a hard matter to live on this earth at all. Look at the savage, and you will see that he can produce no great art or science or literature— no "culture"—because it is all he can do to live. When he has gathered together a little wealth, then he begins to be civilized. But it is still hard for him to live. The rich alone have money enough to pay for art, to pay for artists, and to pay for the toil of other men who will take labour off their shoulders and give them leisure to improve their minds.

It is necessary to face this harsh fact. We need not throw up hands of horror over it; we are in no position to do so. But it is true that the cultivated Chinese, Greek or Roman enjoyed his culture because he was able to command the labour of a huge slave class. Without them the thing we call "civilization" was impossible.

Women's Partnership in the New World

Much of our talk about "honest labour" having a "lovely face" is sentimental. Honest labour—yes, perhaps: but not the grinding toil that crushes the life out of us. Those ant-like workers on the hill outside Nanking could not enjoy the beauty they were creating: they had no time to do so. This truth, which has become horrifying to our modern conscience, must be faced. *No* great civilization has been possible without the sacrifice of the many to the few. We may argue whether the sacrifice is justifiable or not. Philosophers in the past have agreed that it certainly was: philosophers of to-day are uneasy about it. But the fact remains. These great gifts to the world of art and beauty have *always* been made possible by these means, and these means only.

Sometimes the slaves were conquered enemies, sometimes the poorer among the single race, and always they have been women. On them, as on the foreigner and the poor, the labour which made great culture possible has been laid. And, whether we resent it or not, whether we think the culture worth the sacrifice or not, we must admit that it has always been bought at this price. Always.

What then? Must our awakening conscience be put to sleep again? Or must we abandon the idea of a still nobler civilization to come? Or say that civilizations should not be measured by their most glorious achievements but by a higher standard of comfort for the whole population, with no time or money wasted on the costly work of beauty and of art?

These alternatives are unattractive. There is another way.

Many years ago Henry Ford declared his ambition

What Next?

to be to *take the burden of toil off flesh and blood and lay it on steel.*

He had seen the labour of the farmers and labourers of America, working to develop its great spaces and wring their livelihood from its soil. It ought to be an inspiring business. It was in fact a grinding toil. I do not say there was no inspiration in it, for there certainly was, and this inspiration has been the romance of America to whom the "covered wagon" of the pioneers moving westwards has been what sailors and the sea have been to us. But the work of those pioneers can only be described as a grinding toil. To "develop" America's Middle West left the toilers no time or strength for anything else. Ford, whose name will be for ever associated with the first cheap motor car in the world, was not first inspired by the prospect of quick and easy travelling, but by the hope of "lifting the burden of toil from flesh and blood and laying it on steel." His first motor engine was not used for the T model car but for a tractor.

It is an interesting light on human nature that it was not the farm tractor, important as this was, but the cheap car that the farmers wanted. They wanted some power that would lighten their own gigantic toil, it is true, and wanted it badly; but they wanted still more to break the terrible isolation in which many of them lived. The vast spaces of the Middle West, the sparse population, the poverty and toil which made long journeys in a wagon or on horseback out of the question left them with a spiritual need even greater than the material one. They wanted human beings and human intercourse. Every farmer, even if he had no tractor, had a T model Ford car. He had no garage, not even a shed; he left his car at night under a tree—if he had a tree. He could not raise the money to buy even this marvellously cheap contraption: he had a mortgage on it. But go without he would not. And Ford became a millionaire.

Second only to the car came the tractor, and its maker began to realize his first ambition. He took the crushing burden of the world's toil off flesh and blood and laid it on steel.

Among other things that were once regarded as marvellously civilized and are now, because we are unhappy, blamed for our unhappiness, is machinery. The word "machine-made" is now a term of reproach. This machine-made age, this machine-made civilization—with the implied charge that it is not a civilization at all—these jeers go along with an enormous development of machinery and an eager use of it. Everyone has a car or wishes he had; a wireless, a gramophone, a vacuum-cleaner, a bicycle, a mowing-machine. Everyone travels in trains or steamers or aeroplanes. Everyone buys clothes, food, materials that are machine-made. We heap scorn on machinery while we heap its products on ourselves.

We have forgotten—as Mr. Ford himself seems to have forgotten—the real purpose of machinery. It was to lift from us the burden of our toil.

If it really did that, we should have the way of escape from the inhuman dilemma of every civilization up to the present day. We should no longer have to buy our culture at the expense of an incalculable mass of suffering and toil. We should still work, for honest labour *has* a lovely face; but we should be free of the grinding toil that crushes body and spirit alike. It is

What Next?

a matter of importance to women, for their labour has been the hardest, the least regarded and the least rewarded of all. Women in America, who still remember the lives their mothers or grandmothers led in pioneering days, tell me that the toil of the men was surpassed by that of the women. They seemed *never* to rest. And they bore their children with hardly the respite of a day.

It is true that the fall of civilization has been due to many causes, but here is one of them. It is not a wholesome condition of things that buys leisure and beauty for a few at the expense of millions, and being unwholesome it cannot last. It seemed to an earlier age permissible, but no one now can consider it with an easy conscience. If all had at least some leisure, there would be a release of energy and interest which might even cope with and overcome the other ills which still beset our progress. I do not claim that I have "found out the whole answer" if I claim that to give to all the leisure that has never yet been enjoyed but by the few would make possible something new in the way of civilization, something which, because it was more satisfying, would also be more secure.

Here is a very small example of this truth.

When I was living in Poplar, a distinguished actress came down to talk to us of the possibility of founding theatres on the Vic-Wells lines, on a small scale, in many parts of London and other large and small towns. Mr. St. George Heath, then Warden of the Poplar centre of Toynbee Hall,* was present, and, after listening to an eloquent appeal for a more intelligent appreciation of really good plays, he said that the

* Now closed.

89

Women's Partnership in the New World

difficulty lay largely in the fatigue of the audiences. "If we are to interest ourselves in your schemes," he said, "you must interest yourselves in our social conditions." At this the lady made rather a wry face. "That really isn't our business," she said. "Artists must work at their own job. Politics and economics and social reforms are *not* our job. They are yours." "All right," replied Mr. Heath, "but if you are not interested in getting for the workers shorter hours and better conditions, you will have to put up with no audience at all in the pit and gallery, or an audience too tired to be interested in great plays."

Isn't that true? There are quite a number of people in all classes who have vitality enough and brains enough to be "interested in great plays" even when they are very tired. Most of us have not. I well remember my own youthful contempt for older people who said they didn't want Ibsen or even Shakespeare after a hard day's work, but "something to make them laugh."* Now that I too am old and a little tired I am apt to want something to make me laugh also. I have an inexhaustible appetite for Shakespeare, but I confess to a certain shrinking from the grimmer problem or propaganda play. I simply do not want to see Čapek's "Insect Play" or even Shakespeare "in modern dress," since this generally means a production much less exhilarating to the eye than the now contemned achievements of Irving and Ellen Terry. I understand too, though I am not yet sufficiently exhausted to share,

* Shakespeare can do that, but you cannot be sure he is going to. "Oh, I wish it was *The Merry Widow*," said a woman who was obviously "paper," as she sank into her seat for a performance of *Othello*.

What Next?

the preference of some for the cinema over the theatre. It makes much smaller demands on the intelligence—and one's intelligence is apt to sleep when one is tired out. What one wants is a comfortable seat and something going on—something often so idiotic that spectators do not mind whether they come in at the beginning, the middle or the end. They will come in in the middle, sit comfortably (which generally they cannot do in the cheap seats at the theatre) to the end, and then through the beginning back to the middle again. Or, if they are women, they can sit still and go to sleep.

I have seen women do it so often—and so must everyone—as to wonder why they were willing to pay sixpence to do what, one could not help thinking, they might quite well have done for nothing at home. The answer is that they cannot do it at home. The spectacle of a woman *sitting down* in her own house is one that fills the world with horror. Paul Robeson, introducing a song called "Sit down, Sister" to a wireless audience, told us that, if a negress of the poorer classes heard a voice telling her to sit down, she would certainly jump to the conclusion that she was dead and had gone to heaven, since no one in this earthly world was likely ever to ask her to sit down here. Nor is this only true of the coloured woman. During the last war the labour of women to replace men was so urgently needed that all sorts of arrangements were made to release them from some part at least of their home work. In one town that I visited a communal kitchen was one of these, and it was a huge success. The women could order almost any kind of meal from the kitchen and have it delivered at their own homes. Hot drinks in vacuum-flasks and hot food in containers were at their command at the cheapest possible rates. The scheme was worked so well that the women were grateful and the city proud. I visited it again some years later. The communal kitchen had disappeared. Surprised and disappointed, I asked what had happened, and was told by men and women with long faces that it had worked only too well. When the war was over, and the women had gone back to their "own" work, it was found that some of them had conceived such an appetite for leisure that they had actually been seen *sitting down and reading a newspaper*. I shall never forget the horror on the faces of those who reported to me this unexpected sight. It was clear to them that the kitchen must be closed, and closed it was.

Yet, especially now that women are voters, it might have been hailed as a good omen that they should occasionally read a newspaper? Or if it must be assumed by the sort of critics who always take a gloomy view of human nature that the women were merely reading the abysmal idiocies that appear on the "Woman's Page," at least the spectacle of a woman sitting down to do it need not have seemed more shocking than a man doing so to read the betting news? It did, however, shock observers to the core. The kitchen was closed.

So quite a lot of women pay sixpence and sit in a cinema. It is warm in there, and the seat is comfortable; but best of all, it is dark and no one will see that they are women sitting down.

In the old days, when the cinema was cheaper even than now, young people used to speak of having "twopenn'orth of dark." The phrase aroused suspicion

What Next?

in the minds of some: even so, the purpose of the suspected ones was not so nefarious as that of the woman who wanted nothing more than a seat and gladly paid twopence for it—in the dark.

It is not, however, from these visitors that the producers and actors of the screen can hope for a demand for better productions and finer acting. The artist must care for the betterment of conditions outside the cinema if he is to get a better art within. It seems that Mr. Heath was right when he said that, if artists wanted the workers to be interested in a higher standard of play in the theatre, they themselves must not be totally uninterested in the efforts of working men and women to get a higher standard of life in their homes. If it takes all the energy they have to keep things going, themselves alive and their homes intact, they will not—obviously—have energy left over to co-operate in a great work of art. Yet great works of art *need* co-operation. The audience is as necessary as the artists.

It is significant that so many of the names in the *Dictionary of National Biography* come from the middle classes and the more highly skilled ranks of the workers. A quite astonishing proportion come from the sons and daughters of the clergy. The *Dictionary of National Biography* gives us only a rough idea of the people to whose lives and labours we owe most, but still it is worth considering. Those who have won a place there have at least done something which their fellows think worth remembering. We should ask ourselves why so many of them come, for example, from the parsonage and the manse. Is there anything in their circumstances that accounts for it? I think there is.

Women's Partnership in the New World

Capacity for great things is not found in one class only. We received ours from our forefathers, and must make the best we can of our inheritance. But making the best of what we have is a business of the first importance. It seems that to find life too easy is not an incentive, since the character easily softens and the intelligence may suffocate under the weight of great wealth. Too much comfort is not good for the brain.

But neither will the very poor, and least of all the submerged tenth, give us much. Life for them is too hard, as for the rich it is too easy.

In the middle and skilled working classes we find more. Take the parsonage-home, for example. Here are surroundings which are apt to be austere. There is rarely much wealth. There is hardness and a simple way of living. But there is ambition of a right and noble kind. The parents have had a good education and are ready to sacrifice a good deal in order, if it be any way possible, to give the same to their sons. (I say nothing of their daughters, who are often sacrificed to their brothers.) Short of their spiritual welfare, I suppose there is nothing that the average parson cares for more or half as much as this. The boy himself, however, must make efforts. He must live hard, work hard, win scholarships and pay some part of his education himself. He must be willing to be at school and college with boys who have more money and better clothes than himself. These things are not always trifles; they count a good deal in a boy's life. He must put up with them if he is to succeed. Is it surprising after all that the proportion of those who do succeed (as witnessed by the *Dictionary of National Biography*) is so great among the sons of the clergy?

What Next?

The description of the life and standards of the parsonage and manse holds good to a considerable extent of the skilled artisan. He too finds life quite hard enough. He is unlikely to make his children "soft." He is ambitious for them. He wants for them not only as good a chance as he had but a better one. He and his wife are willing to do without their youthful earnings, in order to keep them longer at school and even college.

It seems then that this is what human beings need. A life that is hard but not overwhelmingly hard; the necessities of life in food and clothing, but not suffocating wealth. Admitting that *natural* gifts are as commonly found in one class as another, this conclusion explains the greater proportion of successes in some.

Once more we can see the truth to which our personal experience witnesses on the greater stage of the world.

Not individuals only but nations respond to circumstances in the same way. There are peoples whose lives are so hard that it is all they can do to keep their foothold in life. We may find them decent and praiseworthy people: we shall not find them producing great works of art. They have neither time nor strength for these. The Esquimaux in the north, the Tierra del Fuegians in the south, find living altogether too exacting. The natives of other areas, such as the desert regions of Africa and Australia, are in the same case. In the vast tangle of the jungle life also is very hard, but on the other hand there are tropical countries in which life is only too easy. Men who have nothing to do but scratch the surface of the ground for food or stretch out a hand to pick fruit do not trouble themselves to work. They are content to exist and find our doctrine of the excellence of honest toil ridiculous. They, like the rich man's son, find life too easy and make no progress because they feel no spur. It is chiefly in the temperate places of the world, and not either at the Poles or the Equator, that great civilizations are built up; or if near the Equator, then in areas where heights make the air invigorating but life is not too easy.

We seem bound to the conclusion that a life that is hard but not too hard is the best from which to evoke individual excellence or national achievement. Can we not apply our knowledge?

What is wrong with a machine-made world? Was Ford wrong when he dreamed of taking the load of toil off flesh and blood and laying it on steel? I do not think so. I remember the cost of that toil while it lay altogether on flesh and blood. I recall the stone carvings, the pictured records of old civilizations, showing human beings in an extremity of toil. I see again the antheap outside Nanking. My heart cries out against this horrible disregard of human life, the excess of suffering, the blood and sweat that created the leisure and the wealth of those ancient civilizations. Yet my judgment equally rejects a plan of life in which their glories should be sacrificed to a mere standard of comfort and all alike be toilers and none artists. There is a way out: machinery to do for us the more laborious but necessary toil, and to release us *all* for work less utterly crushing.

Seen from this point of view, machinery is not the curse we are being told to-day that it is. It should be a blessing; but something has gone wrong, for in fact it is a curse. It has not done what it promised. Human

What Next?

beings are still overworked. Machinery has not helped us to produce a great art. On the contrary, it has in many ways cheapened and coarsened both arts and crafts. It has thrown millions out of employment, substituted the dole for a wage or a salary. We have come to think of it as an enemy.

Two of the unemployed watched a great engine scooping out a railway-siding at two tons a scoop. "If it weren't for that there machine," says Jack to Harry, "they'd 'ave to 'ave five 'undred of us men to dig the stuff out with shovels." "Yes," says Harry to Jack; "and if it weren't for shovels, they'd 'ave to 'ave five millions of us digging it out with salt-spoons."

Is that sense? Certainly it is. A shovel may not be machinery, but it is only a step away. It works better than a salt-spoon; that is to say, its use calls for a smaller number of men to dig. But we do not therefore summon five million of unemployed and arm them with salt-spoons! The answer of those who criticize the use of machinery is the answer of the toiling mass of men and women without whose blood and sweat civilization has until now always been impossible. It is a challenge that cannot be ignored or thrust aside with a contemptuous jeer at a "machine-made age." Women who have been the world's drudges, and who are nevertheless the world's individualists, should set themselves to meet it. How shall we do so? Cast aside the machines that are "labour-saving" and let labour once more crush the life out of the masses? Or abandon the hope of recreating a civilization more glorious in art and culture than has ever been known before?

We will do neither? Then we must ask ourselves what machinery is really good for, to what uses it

97   G

ought to be put, and where it should be rigidly excluded.

This is our task—the women's task. If we succeed in it, civilization will once more be born of us.

Let us begin by asking what machinery has done for us that is good. We may notice that even Mahatma Gandhi, whose detestation of nearly all machinery is famous, exempts the sewing-machine. This labour-saving device, he says, was born of love: it was made expressly for the purpose of relieving women of some of their endless toil. But would this not equally justify the use (for example) of the steam-tractor for agriculture, as we have seen Henry Ford meant it to do for men on the land what the sewing-machine was to do for women in the homes? And this is true of the machinery in mines. The conveyor and the little engines that carry the coal about have taken away some of the most odious features of the life underground. Women on all fours, half-naked and with a chain round their waists, were once used to drag the trolleys of coal. Ponies were at last substituted for them; but what lover of animals can think without grief of these attractive little beasts condemned to so unnatural a life in the darkness of the coal-mine? The conscience which was shocked by the employment either of women or of ponies must ask itself the question: Am I prepared to say that the world must do without coal? Or shall I welcome the introduction of machinery into the mine?

Any intelligent person can think of a hundred examples, all showing that machinery has lightened the toil of people whose toil was inhumanly great till it came to their help. I need not labour the point any further.

But the machinery has also, by adding enormously

What Next?

to production, levelled up the standard of life among the poorer people. This is not only good in itself—some perhaps may think that arguable—but it is good in that it removes much of the bitterness of class distinction. It is a commonplace that the working girl to-day wears clothes that wipe out the class distinction of dress altogether. To the expert eye, no doubt, she does not look just like her richest sisters; but she looks, especially if she has the art of wearing her clothes, quite as charming. We have learnt that this art does not only belong to the rich woman but is quite as common and much more important in the professional and working woman. Indeed, I am told that one reason why fashions in dress change with such lightning rapidity nowadays is that the rich are always trying to keep a step ahead of the poor in wearing the latest thing—and finding it very difficult too!

Machine production on a great scale is a democratizing influence. It has destroyed much of the bitterness of class feeling. A man who owned a magnificent car was far more odious to the man who had no car at all than he is to the owner of a little cheap car. At the beginning the possession of a car undoubtedly emphasized and embittered class feeling to such an extent that there was almost a feud between the non-owner and the owner. To-day there is a comradeship of the road between all motorists which is very remarkable and very delightful. Since there are many motorists and many cheap mass-produced cars, there is none of the bitterness of exclusive possession. Everyone hopes that he may own a car some day, and very often indeed his hope is realized. In the meantime he learns all he can about the mechanism of cars, and with a willing and delightful courtesy puts his knowledge of these at the service of less knowledgeable drivers in distress. "It's a poor show if one driver can't help another on the road" has been the answer of many a man when offered a tip for such services. Motorists have a bad enough name, and in view of the frightful number of avoidable accidents on the road they must deserve it; but there is at least this good to be said of them: their democracy includes the Rolls-Royce owner and the driver of a little side-car.

This democratizing trend is present also in the "machine-made" art of the cinema and the broadcast concert. No one who loves a good play can help regretting the turning of hundreds of theatres into cinemas; but in many of them poor plays were very poorly acted, and the cheap seats were uncomfortable to a degree unimaginable in a cinema. There all the seats are comfortable, all have a clear view of the performance, and—more important still—the films are the same for all. The small town which could never hope for a visit from a first-class company of actors has only to wait a few weeks in order to see the greatest film stars in the best plays exactly as they are seen in London. Those who live in small country towns, as I do, can best appreciate this. We do not see the plays quite so soon, but we see them more cheaply. It is at least as broad as it is long. The theatre, in fact, was designed for the rich: the cinema is for rich and poor alike.

The wireless concert follows the same line. No one with an ear for music will say that it comes as perfectly from the radio-set as when heard in the Queen's Hall. There must always be some loss in "canned music."

What Next?

Nevertheless, it is music for all or nearly all. The number of people possessing a wireless of some kind enormously exceeds the number of people able to go to a first-class concert in a great hall. Those who listen at home to a Toscanini, a Beecham, a Henry Wood or an Adrian Boult conducting a B.B.C. concert get something less than those who go to the concert in person; but there are millions instead of hundreds listening, and what they get is very good. For a great proportion of them the choice has not been between superlative music and very good, but between superlative music and none. Indeed, most had no choice at all: for them it was none.

We must also put into the balance the degree of intelligence needed in a mechanical age. The number of people possessing a wireless of some kind is very great. "Of some kind" includes all the home-made sets put together by the listeners themselves. It is a task requiring some skill, and it is generally admirably done. Even to keep a ready-made set in good order is a skilled job, and though many people never acquire it, an increasing number do.

Photography is to the eye what broadcasting is to the ear—a cheap form of art, but still an art. We cannot all have pictures by Turner or portraits by Velasquez: we can all, or nearly all, have photographs. Not so good, nor requiring genius to make them; but often very good indeed, and requiring real talent; and available for all.

I was once sitting in an ambulance post which had been provided by some generous giver with a wireless-set. An account was being given of the adventures of a British submarine which was a romance. To me it

Women's Partnership in the New World

was first and foremost a romance of the daring of men:
to my fellow-drivers, all of whom on that shift happened
to be men and nearly all skilled mechanics, it was most
of all a romance of their skill and excellence as crafts-
men. Again and again these listeners exclaimed at the
marvellous work put into the making of that submarine.
The strains and stresses it suffered as depth-charges
burst all round it were, as they knew better than I,
colossal. If one screw, bolt, nut or rivet had been loose,
one plate flawed, the whole must have been a wreck.
That the men who navigated it should be heroes they
took for granted; of course they were! But those
listeners would heartily have endorsed the tribute I read
afterwards in a newspaper article: "If we may not, for
reasons of safety, yet know the names of the men in
that boat, there is at least one name that deserves
immortal honour, and that we may know—the firm of
Messrs. Cammell Laird, who built it."

To watch men in charge of some great engine is to
see a wonderful thing. The machine itself becomes
beautiful. Its power, swiftness, precision are all glorious.
Its services to man are excellent. Where few indeed
could travel in the old days, many can travel now.
The motor-bus, the train, the car, steam and motor-
boats, aeroplanes have opened the world to us.

Once more there comes the pang of regret. A great
steamboat is a thing of power and beauty; so is an
aeroplane. Neither of them is one half so beautiful as
a great ship in sail.

Let us put in the balance all the skill of the mechanic
and the scientist, all the widespread opportunities of
music and drama, travel and a higher standard of
comfort. On the other side the fact that none of the

What Next?

machine-made things are quite so beautiful or so fine as those laboriously made "by hand" must be weighed. Music is not so perfect, photography immensely inferior, the "canned" drama of the cinema too slick and easy—all these have suffered from machinery. What is wrong with a machine-made civilization? Where ought we to have kept the machine out? And where let it in?

Let us turn back to see what it was for—"to take the burden of toil off flesh and blood." Instead of this it has been used to produce an enormous number of *things*. We have used it as though a man's life consisted in the abundance of the things that he possesses. It does not. An abundance of things is more likely to suffocate than to help him. He who gains the whole world has lost his soul already: he has no time for it. It is possible to have one's house so cluttered up with labour-saving machines that one has no room to breathe. One feels suffocated. At last there is no room for anything and no time but to keep the tiresome things in order. Life suffers in the same way. It gets cluttered up, and so do we. We can hardly move because we have so many things to pack up before we do. We are tied to our possessions—nay, we are buried under them. We are in debt and have mortgaged the future because, in order to possess more and yet more, we must possess on the instalment plan. Our future is in pawn. We even, if we happen to think of him, envy St. Francis, who had nothing but the (very scanty) garments he stood up in; or Gandhi with his cotton loincloth.

During a part of my life, when I was minister at the Guildhouse in London, I spent a lot of time "seeing off" important persons who had been good enough to come and speak to us there. What a to-do! The car was not there, the taxi had not been ordered, the wrong attaché-case was taken—the umbrella—the hat —all seemed in an uproar.

One day Mahatma Gandhi came. When he had spoken he left. He smiled at me and said, "Now I go." And he went. It was as simple as that. He had no coat, no hat, no umbrella, no car, no nothing. As for his cotton loincloth, he referred to it in his speech: "If anyone wants to take it off me, he can: I shall not call in the police." The bodyguard of stalwart policemen with which a paternal Government had insisted on surrounding the Mahatma burst out laughing. So did we all. And how some of us envied him! We have not the strength to face such a heroic poverty. I cannot see how the mother of a family can do without possessions, whatever others may do, even if they are (and many of them are) heroic. Our climate makes voluntary poverty in this stark sense more difficult than a warmer one. All this is true, and yet—we envied him. To be *able* to do without possessions means such a wonderful freedom.

I do not, however, dream of a world inhabited with a race of beings without possessions. What I want to find is how to live with fewer and better ones, and the tendency of the machine age seems all the other way. It creates piles and masses of possessions, but some of them smother their possessors; some are simply wasted because there are "too many" of them—a glut; and of them all *none* go to the people who need them most.

There are innumerable women who never get to a

104

What Next?

cinema, never go for a journey, have no labour-saving machinery in their homes and no leisure in their lives.* The machine age has piled up mountains of things: it has been too busy doing so to consider how to distribute them. In spite of the fact that the general level of life has been greatly raised, it remains true that there are too many slaves still to be found for whom machinery has done little or nothing. Dr. Janet Campbell speaks of "the domestic slavery under which many women live," and adds "for it is nothing less."† Again, she refers to "the almost intolerable weight of unpaid domestic labour"‡ which rests on the wife and mother, "the slave," adds Mrs. Spring Rice, "without whose labour the whole structure of the family tends to collapse."§

"The rationalization of labour has passed over the working mother, leaving her to carry on in more or less the same primitive way that has been customary since the world began."‖

This brings us face to face with our problem. Machinery *might* make civilization a reality by taking on itself the hardest of our labours and by creating goods on such a scale that all could have some leisure and all be "civilized." It has done this to some extent. But there are still slaves—some enslaved by the preposterous mass of their possessions and some, incredible as it may seem, by having too few.

* See *Working-Class Wives*, by Margery Spring Rice, if you cannot believe this, and remember that this book was written in 1939. Not once but many times is recorded the blunt statement: "She has *no* leisure whatever." See especially Chapter V, "The Day's Work."

† Op. cit., p. ix. ‡ Op. cit., p. xi
§ Op. cit., p. 14. ‖ Op. cit., p. 15.

Women's Partnership in the New World

This is because machinery has missed its way, lost sight of its goal. *It was to create leisure: it has only created things.*

Things, if they are the right and necessary things, may create leisure for us certainly: if they are too many and too complicated, they make us more insanely busy than ever. Mass production can make much more tolerable the lives of the masses: it can also debase our taste, impoverish our arts, and make thin and poor the texture of our lives.

No one can draw a rough-and-ready line in such matters. It will be the business of those who build the future to make some decision as to the use and abuse of the machine. Instead of hailing it as a heaven-sent solution of our difficulties or cursing it as the work of the devil, they must harness it to our service and refuse to let it harness us to itself.

I have not written of what seems to many the worst side of the machine age, that is to say, the development of the art of destruction. No wars have so destroyed the very fabric of life as the present wars. None have so broken up homes and destroyed nations. In none have such vast populations been "in the front line" as now, when bombs fall on women and children as indiscriminately as on troops. But this evil use of machinery is a symptom rather than a disease, and the disease lies at least in part in the heaping up of material possessions. Having mass-produced goods on such a scale as leaves their distribution unplanned and uncared for, markets must be sought all over the world. People who did not know of the existence of the things made must be taught to want them. If they do not, there will be a glut at home and millions out of work.

What Next?

The demand for foreign markets, colonies, "spheres of influence," goes hand-in-hand with the threat of unemployment, and both contribute to the making of wars. These in their turn create a demand for guns, bombs, tanks, high explosives and all the ghastly machinery of war. We cannot separate machinery, mass production, unemployment and war: they form a vicious circle from which the world must escape or perish.

We should insist that the machine be used not primarily to create *things* but to create *leisure*. Instead of speeding up our lives, it should slow them down. Instead of using (for example) a motor car in order to squeeze in three engagements where in the age of the horse we could only have kept one, we should use it in order that the *one* may not take up a whole day but only a small part of it and leave some leisure round it. This is not easy, for we have lost not only the use of leisure but even the sense of it. If we have it, we feel guilty. Like the women who shocked their fellow-citizens by sitting down, we are conscious of surprise and contempt in our friends if we admit that we have some free time on our hands. To be smilingly accused of "never taking a holiday" or of being continually overworked to the verge of exhaustion is to be aware that a compliment is intended. How silly this is, and what an inhuman existence it suggests!

The most exasperating form of request is to me the request that one should undertake more work on the grounds that "it is always the busiest people who can find time for one more undertaking." No doubt it is. The busiest people have by now lost the power to sit still. They are thrown into a fever if they have to do so for ten minutes. They complain that so-and-so has caused them to waste ten minutes, and they are right, for it *is* wasted. They have no idea of making use of it in quietness.

I have travelled a good deal in Canada and the United States. It requires more than a surgical operation to persuade the people of these countries that I *prefer* to travel by day. To travel by nights means to sleep in positive misery, amid deafening noises, snores, clatter, bangs, and the clangour of an enormous bell* as one roars through wayside stations. It is to go to bed in discomfort and to dress without a bath. When asked why Americans prefer this horrid experience, they reply at once "to save time." If you say that, for your part, you prefer to sleep by night and travel by day so that you can see the country you are passing through and perhaps even pass the time of day with your fellow-travellers, they do not believe you.

Here in England it sometimes happens that, in spite of the most strenuous efforts not to "waste" ten seconds of our time, the programmes of the B.B.C. do not perfectly fit. The announcer, horror-stricken, admits

---

* The trains in America are of colossal size. They make such a din that the earth shakes at their approach. It is like an earthquake or a tornado, or both. Round the neck of each engine is hung a bell, which is rung as it passes through a station. Standing on the platform of a wayside station I was, as usual, deafened by the sound of an approaching train. My curiosity about the bell, however, overcame my disinclination to raise my voice above the uproar. I yelled to a friend, "What is the bell for?" I had to repeat this yell several times before my friend could hear what I was asking. When at last he grasped my meaning he said with surprise, "To let people know the train is coming."

What Next?

that "the next item of the programme is not due for—
er—one and a half minutes. I think we have *just* time
for a record." No doubt he knows his audience. It
would be frightful if we had to sit quiet for one and
a half minutes.

When I think of those women who have literally *no*
leisure* and no labour-saving machinery to provide
them with it, it seems to me a kind of insanity that
other women (and men) should use machinery merely
to make leisure more and more impossible for themselves. When I think further that slavery was defended
by great and splendid people on the ground that it was
absolutely necessary for civilization that some should
have leisure for the arts and could not have it without
the inhuman toil of slaves, I am still more amazed to
find that humanity now has a slave that is not human
and that cannot suffer—and uses it to destroy leisure
altogether!

It is a platitude to say that man has become the
slave of his own machines, but it has not ceased to be
a tragedy. It is besides an unnecessary tragedy. We
need not produce on so vast a scale that what is produced has to be wasted. We *need* not give all our minds
to producing things so that we have no minds left but
only things. We *need* not. No arguments from financiers,
manufacturers or business men should impress us when
we remember that they have between them—and us,
for we have our share of responsibility—created a world
in which (*a*) we can produce plenty for everybody,
(*b*) much of what we produce is wasted, and (*c*) millions
have practically no possessions at all. In fact, a lunatic
asylum.

* See *Working-Class Wives*, as above.

Women's Partnership in the New World

I have quoted many times and with deep appreciation the words of Henry Ford, who proposed to himself the noble aim of lifting from flesh and blood the crushing burden of toil and laying it on steel. I have not quoted it once without remembering the men I saw in Detroit coming from his great factories, exhausted with that labour. I have not forgotten the bitter complaints on every side of the inhuman speed and drive of the work there. I have not forgotten the masses of the unemployed who were laid off during the great turnover from one type of car to another. Mr. Ford set a standard through all America of high wages and short hours for his workmen: but the machine got the better of him, made him and them its slaves, and, in spite of hours and wages, its slaves they are.

So too are we, for we allow ourselves to be hypnotized by the mass-produced things where they are out of place. Again it is, of course, a matter of drawing the line. Still, it may be that it is our business to draw it. How many of the things in our own home must be machine-made? How many would not be longer-lived and more beautiful if they were made by hand? Furniture? Books? Utensils? Some yes, some no. I confess I do not know, but I believe that we should aim at a higher standard of use and beauty and be content with a lesser number of things. We are already on the way. The average house is bare and bleak compared with that of a past generation. People have fewer "ornaments" and wear fewer clothes than they did. It is all to the good, both for our houses and our bodies. Having gone a little way, let us go further.

One book bought when we have found it good, one visit to the theatre instead of six to the cinema, one

What Next?

beautiful if "useless" thing to look at—china, glass or wood—instead of a number of the cheap horrors we see in "gift shops" and the like. Above all, some hours at least for leisure that we may savour that book, theatre or other work of art.

Machinery for the most grinding toil, for transport—for what else? I do not know; but I am sure that it should be above all for leisure—not for things; and for things only so far as they create leisure.

I appeal to women to solve the problem of the machine-made age, for they have been the world's worst drudges and it is for them to rebel. Let not that which should be our salvation turn to our destruction.

Chapter V

The Value of Women's Experience of Life

WHEN a baby is conceived its growth is unconscious, and the share of the mother's body in that growth is to a certain extent involuntary. When it is born she has greater freedom to choose how she shall serve it, and as it grows up it gains freedom too and can co-operate or not with its parents' plans for it.

It is the same with the race. When women chose a settled rather than a wandering life, they did not really exercise much conscious choice, and they had no idea what a momentous decision they were making. They acted as they did because it was their nature to do so as the mothers of children. The men acquiesced because the choice was really in accordance with their natures too.

After uncounted ages of the rise and fall of civilizations, however, we can and must make more conscious choices. If we are to overcome the difficulties which have led to these falls, we must use our intelligence. By "we" I here mean, of course, both men and women; but, since I believe that the next move lies with women, I must ask myself what prevents us from using our intelligence more to the purpose than we are doing. Two things stand in our way. One is our lesser muscular strength which, in a world of violence, makes us dependent on men: the other is the unfortunate willingness of women who rebel against this dependence to depise their own sex.

The Value of Women's Experience of Life

The first obstacle is easy to understand. Civilizations have always been based largely on force of arms, ability to defend oneself and the State and to keep order inside it. It has been based on other and more spiritual forces, but these are invisible and easily pass unnoticed. So to the sex which has superior physical strength has belonged the prestige of a governing class. Men have naturally assumed their superiority over women, and women have cordially agreed with them. This robs us of self-confidence and makes it easy for us to believe that our work, our needs and, above all, our ideas are less important than men's.

The second obstacle is more surprising at first sight. It is that among the "rebel" women there has been an equal or even greater readiness to think the work of women rather contemptible. Red-hot feminists were so determined to be "equal" with men that they proceeded to act as though only men were enviable or respectable. To suggest that women's needs should be equally considered and their work regarded as equally important was to enrage these feminists and to be set down by them as reactionary. One of the most brilliant women in the feminist movement was exasperated by the—after all, very natural—tendency of League of Nations' authorities to put the few women ever appointed as delegates on to the Commissions which dealt with subjects which they innocently supposed to be those for which women specially cared and of which they knew most. The traffic in women and children is an example. "Women's worries" was the contemptuous phrase used by this critic. Are women's worries then not worth considering? Or were such horrors as these not worth their worry?

H

Women's Partnership in the New World

By all means let women who have a special knowledge of other matters be put on to Disarmament Conferences, Courts of Arbitration and the like, and by all means let us women have all the opportunities that we want for equipping ourselves with such knowledge; but let us recognize the fact that women who excel in these matters will always be the exception and women who excel in "women's worries" the rule, and that this is not a thing to despise or to regret.

To think of the man in the house as the "breadwinner" and of the woman as his "dependent" is really idiotic. The woman who spends is "winning" the family bread as truly as the man, and he and his children are as "dependent" on her as she on him. To say that one is more important than the other is senseless. They are as equal as the two blades of a pair of scissors. It has been a great misfortune that both men and women should have agreed to think that one blade is more important than the other, because it is not true and the idea has made our civilization lopsided. And it is again a misfortune because it has deprived women of the confidence in themselves and their opinions that they so greatly need to-day.

The enormous majority of women would rather do their own work than any other, and by "their own work" I mean quite definitely and unashamedly the work of a wife and mother in a home. I assert this, and it is one of the few things in this shaky world that I am absolutely sure of. Of course no woman should be assigned this job against her will, and of course there are women who are born celibates. There are also women who are born scientists, artists, administrators, teachers, statesmen and so forth. There will always be

The Value of Women's Experience of Life

real suffering if the State or public opinion tries to force these women into a domesticity that does not suit them, and real loss to us all of their services in what does suit them. Moreover, the refusal of liberty of choice of a career to women naturally makes them suspect that they are required to do their own job not because it *is* their job but because it is too dull or too unimportant for men to want to do it. To use either physical or economic strength in order to limit people's development in any direction is a stupid and disastrous thing to do. People have a right to develop along their own lines, and this is true of all people, and women are people.

If we had been expected to develop our own gifts without anyone telling us beforehand what they ought to be, there would have been none of the exaggerated admiration on the part of "advanced" women for occupations which on the whole suit men best,* and none of the unfortunate tendency of the same women to think of those which on the whole suit women best as second-rate and unimportant.

Women are the world's individualists, and should be a nation's and a world's strongest bulwark against mass production and mass thinking; therefore against the totalitarian State. Yet there is no doubt that both Fascism and Nazism† have made quite a strong appeal to them. I believe this to be due to the recognition

* Some feminists even demand the right of women to serve in the Army and Navy—not as at present in the auxiliary services, but in the ranks as fighting units.

† I do not here include Communism because, though equally totalitarian, its treatment of women has been far more generous and enlightened, so that its appeal to them is very understandable.

Women's Partnership in the New World

given by their leaders to the national importance of women's work. Motherhood has been exalted in the past, but generally in a sentimental way, and it has been coupled with severe restrictions on women's activities and an implied opinion that they are not, in spite of sentiment, really important people—if indeed they are people at all. When the slowing down of the birthrate first became a "men's worry," President Roosevelt* was told that the man he was shaking hands with was the father of twelve (or fourteen or twenty, I forget which) children, and he led the applause that followed and shook hands with this prolific father all over again. This is saying a lot, since more than one American President has had his right hand put out of action by devotion to the duty of every American President to shake hands with everybody who wants to shake it.† For my part, I was enraged at this misdirected enthusiasm. Who had had the babies, anyway?

Totalitarian Germany and Italy have been less sentimental but much more sincere in their appreciation of the person who has the baby. After a period of scolding and lecturing on the subject of large families, both dictators and women began to see the matter in a different light. I cannot do better than quote the words of a woman (and a feminist in the truest sense), Miss E. Pick, who writes in the *International Women's News*:‡

"It is a piece of elementary psychology that the subjugated mind and spirit tries to find a way out of its

* Not the President Roosevelt now in office, but the "Teddy" Roosevelt of the beginning of the century.
† The population of the U.S.A. is about 120 or 130 millions.
‡ July and August 1940.

116

The Value of Women's Experience of Life

oppression, so one must not be surprised that since 1918 women have found their way in all European countries into those groups where *they were made to believe they were efficient and important*,* and thus became the most obedient and faithful adherents of Fascism and Communism. The Fascist movement is based on the belief in racial superiority. Here women were no second-class citizens, but were esteemed as mothers, sisters, educators of the future superman. They had special work in organization and instruction, and *their work had a special prestige** which glorified the dull work, even house and needlework, to which they were in reality condemned. They learned to see it in another light: the light of their own efficiency. One cannot compare women's attitude with that of men, even though we know that the mass of men too may be seduced to join such a movement by their own inferiority complex. But women were acting against the laws of womanhood, against their natural feeling, against their own instinct, *because the past had made them a sort of amphibia, with rights and duties that remained dubious and uncertain."**

This is most justly stated, and it is because the older generation of women (to which I belong) did not understand it that, as Miss Pick says, they "failed to win the younger women."

Fascism, Nazism, Communism, all alike "act against the laws of womanhood" both in their use of violence and in their disregard of the individual. But so do those women who would relegate "women's worries" to a secondary position and try to build the new civilization on the assumption that it is the men's job that is the really important and really enviable one.

I have spoken of the slavery of women to their tasks in our poorer homes. But this slavery, all women know,

* The italics are mine.

117

is lightened and consecrated by the knowledge that it is in the service of the people most dear to them. This feeling has been and still is abominably exploited, and the sense of the beauty of home life cannot endure where the exploitation is too gross and cruel; but it is true that there *is* a beauty and dignity in personal service given in love that is absent from the more crushing forms of male industry, and the women know it and are well aware of the difference. It is no use to tell them that their job is of secondary importance. They may let this thought influence them too much when they ought to speak out; but in their hearts they resent the attempt of well-meaning reformers to make them "a sort of amphibia with rights and duties that remain dubious and uncertain."

However great the prestige of men, women deep in their hearts know that the "woman's job" in the home is at least equally important. Their resentment against a few women who think contemptuously of it may be measured by the fact that they have in such large numbers accepted Fascism and Nazism, although they violate their own natures in doing so. If the democracies want to win the same enthusiasm, they must not be content to set women free *in theory* to take up other work if they choose: they must revolutionize the conditions under which at present the work in the home is too often done. It must not only be honoured in sentimental songs and phrases but in deed and in truth.

In return women will give their devotion to a form of government which does not violate their natures by making children into the puppets of the State as Fascism demands. They will rejoice in the freedom of the children for whom they travail to develop according

The Value of Women's Experience of Life

to the gifts they have and along their own lines. But it must be a real freedom, economic as well as political. We must not be told that both we and our children *may* do what we think best, because "there is no law against it": we must be sure that we *can* do it, because good houses, good schools and colleges, more leisure, better provision for the sick, a higher standard of living for all but those whose standard is too high already, make it possible. Let us find courage to ask for the things we really want and the principles in which we really believe, without being silenced by the fear that we do not know enough to ask wisely or to believe rightly. We know what is right in our homes. We know that what is true on the small scale will be true also on the great scale.

Let us take courage.

Chapter VI

What Do People Really Want?

IF a woman who has a husband and a family of children does not know a lot about human nature, she has missed her job and ought to be in a factory where she can deal with machines instead.

But most women do know quite a lot. It is time we brought our knowledge into the open. We are making enormous efforts now to win the war. What then? What do we really want? Suppose we win a victory as overwhelming as in 1918? We did not do much good with it then, since we meant to put an end to war for ever and now are at war again. What can we do now, to clear our own minds?

Take the average boy and girl that we have in our own homes. What do they want? They want decent homes and as much schooling as they can take. They want work that suits them, that is to say, work that they are fitted to do, that interests them and that is worth doing. They want to marry. They want to have children in course of time—and when I say in course of time I do not mean in course of ages! They want to marry while they are young and to have children while they are young, and in a home which *is* a home, not a box of bricks held together by the wall-paper and paid for on the instalment system. They want to give the children a better world than they had themselves. And they want to be well—fit and strong and sound.

What then? A great many people would be satisfied

What Do People Really Want?

with that, if we include all that is involved in it. Some want more.

The young want adventure. There are glorious adventures left in the world. There are places unreached, like the top of Mount Everest; unexplored, like Central South America. There are huge gaps in our knowledge that can be filled only by the daring of men who will adventure in Polar regions or tropical forests; or again in the researches of medicine. Science has its martyrs and its saints, "voyaging on strange seas of thought alone." Human beings have to be served. The Christian religion must be preached in the face of danger from man as well as nature.

Even in their play many people prefer the risky and adventurous kind. They would rather play football than watch it, rather climb the Alps than hike along the countryside, rather photograph a charging hippopotamus than a sitting friend. I heard of a burglar who, though gaoled several times, "converted" several times, provided with a good job several times, could not refrain from burgling. Why not? Because he found it so gloriously exciting! Had he been a richer man he would have been a big-game hunter, or better still (I hope) a big-game cine-photographer.

Or they—these boys and girls of ours—may want a chance of leadership: they may have a gift for it, and it irks them if that gift is thrown away.

What is wrong with these wants? Or unreasonable? Nothing.

And yet most of us would think we had got All Heaven and This Beside if we could have them. Just to be fit and in a good job and not bothered to death about our friends who are not, and free to marry and to have children and—all the rest of it. It really is very modest, and yet it would be the kingdom of heaven on earth to most of us.

Why do we let ourselves be persuaded that we want quite different things? What difference does it really make to us that we should have—let us say—Togoland? We did not have it before the last war and were, so far as I know, perfectly happy without it. Or if we were not happy, it was not because we had not got Togoland. How many of my readers know where it is, or how big it is, or how many people live in it, or what colour their skins are, or what sort of a place it is? How many even know that we have a mandate for it?

We let ourselves get all worked up about it and feel we must shed the last drop of our blood rather than give it up. All the time we should do far better to remember that, whatever the Togoians are, they are human beings; and find out what *they* want to happen to Togoland.

Do we want friends or enemies? Friends every time. How do you make friends? Certainly not by taking it for granted that if they want something that is ours it is because they are thoroughly wicked people and ought to be smashed. Very likely they want it, whatever it is, for exactly the same reason that we want it. That cannot be wicked then, can it? Perhaps it could be shared? Or given to the one that needed it most? Or perhaps, if we didn't smash things up and waste them in the process of fighting it out, we should find that there was really enough for us both? It often does happen that way.

What all this amounts to is that, taking it for granted that what we want is friendship and not hate, we

What Do People Really Want?

should lay ourselves out to make nations our friends in the same way that we make friends with our neighbours and a friendly atmosphere in our homes. And surely we *can* take it for granted? Most people like to see the world. I think myself very lucky that I have seen so much of it as I have, but there are lots of places I have not seen and should like to. I cannot. Travel is made impossible by war. Isn't it ridiculous that science has made it possible to travel more quickly and more cheaply than ever in the world before, and international hatreds have made it impossible for us to travel at all?

I noticed that among the promises made by Hitler to the young people of Germany was one that, if he and they could only manage to destroy the British Navy, they would be able to travel freely all over the world, as the British Navy was the only thing that stood in the way. Apart from the silliness of this, it is interesting to notice that German boys and girls *want* to travel just as English boys and girls do, and Hitler knows it. They may enjoy seeing other countries all the more for being sure their own is best, but that is not peculiar to Germans, is it? I know the best moment in all my travels is the one that sees me back in England, and I should be sorry for anyone who could not say "East or West, home is best." I am almost as sorry for anyone who knows nothing but home and does not want to. We shall all be in that case soon, if we cannot make friends with the rest of the world.

A great deal of nonsense is talked about the glory of ruling over other nations. It does tickle one's vanity, of course, but it does not really make twopennyworth of difference to our real happiness. On the other hand it makes a lot of difference to theirs and, if we want

123

a friendly world, we ought to remember this and act accordingly. It makes a difference to us whether our parents use the power they have over us to help us to grow up, or to keep us in leading-strings. Neither parents nor elder brothers and sisters should tyrannize over younger ones. Nothing makes for resentment and bitterness more than this. We ought to be as proud to see our children wanting to stand on their own feet intellectually and morally as every mother is to see her baby "feeling its feet" and wanting to run. If we cannot feel that pride, we are not good parents and are likely to stunt and warp the natural development of our children.

Nations should no more want to rule over others than parents to rule their children when they are grown up. How can we know when the time has come? Are you not inclined to believe that a child should be allowed to feel its feet as soon as it really wants to? That is how we can know the time has come for it. He or she should be given freedom and responsibility also when he or she begins to reach out for it. You keep an eye on your children at first: a toddler is not allowed out of your sight to toddle wherever it likes before it has learnt how to walk, and your children have perhaps a small allowance of money before they have complete independence in their spending. But it all comes about naturally and gradually if parents are wise.

When should the "backward"* people be set free

* The word "backward" is nearly always used by British people to mean politically inexperienced, and it is in that sense that I use it here. I am, however, well aware that the politically experienced nation is often spiritually or aesthetically the backward one.

What Do People Really Want?

from tutelage by older ones? Just as with the children. The process should begin as soon as it is asked for, and proceed as the demand grows.

It is one of the most gratifying signs of the times that, during the last few years,* *complete* freedom has been granted to our great Dominions and to Eire— freedom so complete that they decide for themselves whether they are at war with those with whom we are at war, or not. We do not always realize this makes our "empire" entirely different from any other, not only in the past but in the present. No other empire is a Commonwealth of Nations, as we have a right to call ours.

It is a great achievement. Is it not also a proof that the family way is the best way for the nations too?

Why not go further? India has claimed her right to freedom for a long time now. It is as stupid to deny it as to deny to any member of the family the right to grow up. This was brought home to me with great force by a question put to me by a young Indian woman a few years ago. She was a keen nationalist and a brilliant student of history and of international affairs. She and her husband had both been in prison more than once for sedition against the British Government. And this was her question:

"Why are you not proud of us?"

What is your answer? Spiritually India is ahead of us. Politically she has been our child. We have taught her to believe in democratic ideals. Now she is claiming the right to practise them for herself. Why are we not proud of her? We are proud of our own children's growth. Let us rejoice in hers.

A thing of which we can be proud also is the way

* Since the passing of the Statute of Westminster, 1924.

in which far more inexperienced peoples are standing by us now. Dr. Harold Moody* reproaches some who pride themselves on their liberal ideas for their readiness to "give" colonies in Africa and elsewhere to Germany or to place them under international control. He claims that they have a right to remain British if they choose, and believes that they would so choose if they were consulted. That is a legitimate source of pride for us. But Dr. Moody is a keen critic of our colonial government, all the same. He too asserts that the politically inexperienced should be given independence *when they begin to want it* and as quickly as possible. All government, at home and abroad, should be with the purpose of helping people to grow up and taking pride in their growing. We should never want to make Peter Pans of other peoples and should be ashamed of them if they show no sign of growing up—or rather ashamed of ourselves, as parents should be, and generally are, of children whose development they themselves have thwarted.

Even "enemy" nations should be considered as potential friends. The world will never be as we want it to be if we try to force our ideas and our institutions on them. We think our ideas are best? Certainly, and I for my part am quite sure of it. I believe in democracy and loathe totalitarianism for all the many reasons I have set down. But I believe that we shall persuade the world to agree with us only by showing our ideas in practice and in all sincerity. We shall not do so if we are not sincere in accepting them ourselves, or accepting them only for white people, or for certain classes of people in our own land.

* Founder and President of the League of Coloured Peoples.

What Do People Really Want?

There is much that can be done now and without waiting till the war is over. We cannot *now* compel Germany, Italy, Russia or Japan to be democratic—if indeed true democracy ever can be "compelled." But it cannot: the moment we try to compel it we have ceased to be democratic. It is an obvious impossibility to compel people to be free! We can, however, be far more free ourselves than we are yet, and grant freedom where we have hitherto refused it even now.

Let us ask ourselves what we want for our own children, and then demand it for all the children in our Empire. Let us ask what we want for ourselves, and then demand it for everyone else over whose lives we have power.

It takes some thought. Our wants, at first sight, are not the same; so how can we judge what others want? A child wants a toy on its birthday; a grown-up person a book or a machine. An Esquimaux wants a fur coat; a dweller in the tropics hates the sight of it. We all want different things.

But we all want them in the same way. We want, in short, what suits our need. There we are all alike. If we judge the world's wants as we judge our friends', we shall not go far wrong.

The person who gives us the best birthday presents takes a tremendous amount of trouble over the business. He does not walk into a shop and say, "I want a present." He is not satisfied even to add "for my wife" or "for a little girl." He (or should I here say *she*?) reflects that the little girl in question is four years old, has already got all the Teddy Bears she wants, is too young to be interested in a new frock or a lipstick, but has never been known to have all

127

the chocolates she could really eat without serious discomfort.

Generally speaking, men are not such good present-givers as women. Perhaps this too is significant. A present needs to be individual, and "women are so personal" in their feelings. It is a good quality when it comes to giving presents.*

Let us repeat it on the national scale. All nations do not want the same institutions or ways of government. True: but all want *what they want*, and not what we think they ought to want. Some think (for example) that politically backward people *ought* to want to be governed under an international mandate and are deaf to their cries that they would prefer British rule:† others are so sure that they prefer British rule that they are careful not to ask them whether they would not rather rule themselves. Yet others suppose that what the subject peoples wanted once they will always want, which is as though one's godparents should insist on giving one a silver mug every year to infinity. One can, however, write to the erring godfather and be sure he gets the letter: those addressed by discontented peoples to "mandatory powers" seem to be always lost in the post.

Let me once more urge my sister-women everywhere to realize that women do know something about human nature; that they have *had* to know something about

* I do not forget the dreadful courage with which some insane women insist on choosing their husband's cigars and ties; but, while blushing for my sex on this point, I maintain that they are nevertheless and on the whole wiser present-givers than men. And I *have* known a man choose a hat for his wife—heaven help her!

† See above, page 126.

What Do People Really Want?

human nature; and that they don't think of it as "human nature" at all, but as husbands and sons and daughters, all different, all endearing and all immensely important to themselves, to us and to each other: and that that is the right way to think of "peoples" and "nations" and even "great powers."

Women are born democrats. I do not mean that they are not snobs—there are as many female as male snobs, and who has not heard her voice change when she found that the shabby old woman she was talking down to was a duchess?* What I mean is that women have the root of the matter in them. For democracy is not a form of government, nor is it a matter of votes. It is a true sense of the value of the individual. It is a conviction that the State and all its institutions exist for the sake of the individual, and not the individual for the State. The difference between the democratic and the totalitarian State is summed up once for all when we have said this. Everything else follows from it or is of less importance.

Mr. H. G. Wells, in a book written years ago, before the barbarous word "totalitarianism" had been invented, gave us a picture of the total State which cannot be bettered.† He places it in the Moon and devises a plan by which two men from the earth visit it and describe its nature. In the Moon-State the individual counts for nothing. Rulers, scientists, soldiers, mathematicians, machine-minders, mothers—all are appointed to their tasks and have no choice about it,

* Naturally this does not happen often because there are so few duchesses to talk to. Most of us live and die without having talked to even one.

† H. G. Wells, *The First Men in the Moon.*

I

no chance of developing into anything else than that which is appointed them.

"In the Moon every citizen knows his place. He is born to that place, and the elaborate discipline of training, education and surgery he undergoes fits him at last so completely to it that he has neither ideas nor organs for any purpose beyond it . . ." "With a perfect psychological skill" the brain of the citizen who is to be a mathematician is stimulated and trained in such a manner that it grows greatly, but only in its mathematical faculties. "The rest of him only so much as is necessary to sustain this essential part of him." The ruler has his brain even more enormously developed. He and the other intellectuals of the Moon have succeeded in getting rid of their skulls, "that strange box of bone that clamps about the developing brain of man, imperiously insisting 'thus far and no farther' to all his possibilities."

In like manner the machine-minder was from birth "confined in a jar from which only the fore-limbs protruded," the hand in "this highly developed system of technical education" being stimulated and nourished while the rest of the body was starved. It may interest women to know that "the mothers of the Moon world —the queen-bees as it were of the hive"—are "noble-looking beings fantastically and sometimes quite beautifully adorned, with a proud carriage, and, save for their mouths, *almost microscopic heads*."* Mothers in the totalitarian State are not required to have brains.

* The italics are mine.

Chapter VII

The Problems of Sex

BEFORE the outbreak of war no problems were more eagerly discussed than the problems of sex. If for the moment discussion has ceased, it is not because the problems have been solved but because they are shelved. They will remain until they are solved, and war is likely to add to their difficulty.

Looking back over the period 1918–39, that is to say, the years between the two wars, certain tendencies are strongly marked. One is the tendency (it is still only a tendency) to insist on an equal standard of sex morals for men and women which is not that demanded for women in the past but that accepted for men at all times.* Far-sighted people were not surprised at this, and some even think a single low or lowish standard better than a double one. The double standard could not survive the claim of women to equality with men, and it has always involved an amount of lying, hypocrisy and cruelty which the most promiscuous sex relations could not equal. It seems obvious now, but it did not seem obvious to many excellent people in the past, that to insist on physical chastity for one sex and not the other *compelled* the existence of prostitutes, for men cannot be unchaste alone. Certain other things, equally obvious to-day, have to be recognized too. For example, that if prostitutes are necessary they should

* Individual men and women, small sections of the community, or short periods in a nation's history do not here concern me.

not be despised: that if men buy and women sell, the buyer is no more innocent and no more honourable than the seller: that to attempt to protect one of two parties to an immoral act from the danger of disease, and not the other, is both unjust and futile.

I do not intend to discuss these matters: they are obvious. Even if the exigencies and brutalities of war fog the issue for a time, it will clear itself later. It is useless to argue about them, because the argument is too one-sided and those who cling to a discredited morality [sic] do so not because they can reasonably defend it but because they are silly with panic.

There are other more important and permanent trends of opinion. These are largely the result of the universal interest of the present generation in psychology.

It is said that women, like men, are strongly sexed, and that to deny them sexual satisfaction because they happen not to be married is a cruel repression which cannot reasonably be defended. It is pointed out that not all women have the maternal instinct and that—again like men—some are better lovers than parents. The two things are psychologically quite separate and should not be confused in practice. There are women who want sexual intercourse without motherhood and women who want motherhood though they have little or no sexual desire.

If this is so—and who can doubt it?—it is preposterous, we are told, to organize our future society on the assumption that lovers should marry and found families. Quite possibly this does not suit them at all, and therefore it should not be forced upon them. Marriage, it is said, was made for human beings and not human beings for marriage.

The Problems of Sex

This is true. It is time we realized its truth for all human relations and for marriage among the rest. But it is also time that we paused to weigh the implications of this particular and vitally important institution before deciding light-heartedly to scrap it. It is old. It has persisted throughout the ages. It has taken innumerable forms, and in principle survived them all. Neither the group marriages of some primitive peoples, nor polygamy,* nor polyandry,† nor monogamy, nor even divorce has solved all its problems; but neither have any of these expedients destroyed the faith of humanity in *some* form of stable relationship between men and women which we can call marriage.

Perhaps our fundamental mistake is that we seek a human relationship without any of the difficulties of a human relationship. To show that marriage is often very difficult, that its claims become a nuisance and that a nuisance *is* a nuisance, is to say no more than the truth. Indeed, the difficulties of marriage are so undeniable that its continued existence provokes wonder that it should ever have been tried or, if tried, why not quickly discarded? Its obstinate persistence must have some cause.

I shall discuss here only the form of marriage which in the West we have aimed at for centuries, which I believe to be the best, and which I also believe is the one that Christ taught—monogamy. I shall even be bold enough to add that a man and woman should not only be faithful to one another in marriage but celibate before it.

I shall certainly not be bold enough to claim that

* Marriage of one man to more than one woman.
† Marriage of one woman to more than one man.

this sort of marriage is an easy matter. Still less will I denounce those who do not agree with me or, though they agree, find that circumstances have made their marriages or their celibacy a failure; or deny to them relief. Marriage *is* made for humans, and not humans for marriage. But I do believe that faithful monogamous marriage is the ideal to be aimed at, and I face the awkward fact that the attainment of an ideal is never easy.

This is an awkward fact, because the lesson learnt by many students of psychology to-day is that it is dangerous and wrong to attempt what is not easy or, as they say, "natural." To do so is to create repression and to make a failure of life, which should be lived spontaneously and freely. The masters of psychology do not teach this easy creed, but the students have nevertheless learned it. It is fair to blame at least some of the teachers for not warning their disciples with sufficient clearness that they were guilty of a careless misunderstanding.

Let us look closely at the difficulties in the way of monogamy.

There are men and women who are "naturally" polygamous, or, to put it more clearly, naturally unfaithful. They tire of their partner in marriage and wish for a change. They feel it intolerable that they should be expected to give their bodies to one another when their spirits are no longer in accord, or to deny this physical union to someone with whom they are in accord. Or they say that the physical union is a small matter and much too much importance is given to it by old-fashioned moralists. They say besides that both men and women vary in their spiritual and physical

The Problems of Sex

needs and one desires loverhood and another parent-
hood, and to insist that these two needs must always
go together is to fly in the face of human nature.

There is much truth in these contentions, and I do
not base the different conclusion I draw from them on
any attempt to disprove their force. What I want is to
show the worth of monogamy in spite of them. I do
this because I utterly disbelieve the idea that *any* human
relationship can be easy, and I know that the closer
and deeper the relationship is the more it costs.
Marriage, being closest of all, is always going to cost
the most. It costs us our lives. It costs us our lives
even if we do not marry.

This sounds ridiculous, but it is true.

Love is an art, and the most difficult of all arts. It is
the art of life itself. One must not begin by wasting on
trifles the vital energy that will be needed to make it
a success. One must practise it diligently and from the
beginning. Those who accept and enjoy the passing
physical impulse of sex are wasting their own vital
forces. But they have not enough to waste and yet
succeed later on. Life is hard. Not one person has too
much vitality for its demands—not one. The best will
only have just enough. Sex is a most vital form of vital
force, but only one form. Creation on the physical
plane—the procreation of children—is the most universal way of using it, but it is only one way. We all
need all our energy to live well, and we must learn to
use it with force and direction in its various forms. But
we must not waste it, for that is not use at all.

Promiscuous sexual intercourse is not only a waste
of nervous energy: it is a demoralizing habit. It is a
mistake to suppose that those who practise it can, when

they decide to marry and form a stable connection—
probably because they want children and realize that
children need stability—*become* stable overnight. They
have lost the capacity. Yielding to a passing attraction
what is the very sacrament of love has become a habit,
and habit second nature. Such second nature may be
overcome by a great and serious passion, but its over-
coming makes more difficult an achievement which its
critics have already assured us is almost impossibly
difficult already.

Men and women are not always naturally parents
and naturally lovers. Psychology has made known a
fact which would always have been obvious enough if
it had not been obscured by the convenient assumption
that women are all born with a strong maternal
instinct. They are not. Nor are men all born with a
paternal one. Since this is so, why associate loverhood
with marriage? It is generally conceded that children
do need a stable home, and that those who wish to
have children should face the fact and accept a stable
relationship, at least as long as the children are quite
young. Why demand more?

Because what is *apparently* psychologically true is not
physiologically so. Sexual intercourse can be had without children, but children cannot be had without
sexual intercourse. A generation which has gone slightly
mad about "modern psychology" has forgotten this
bald fact. It is, however, quite as important and
significant as the other. Its significance is that what is
true on one plane is true on all in spite of seeming;
what is true of our bodies is true of the rest of us.
There is a psychological truth here. The union of
bodies cannot be only a union of bodies: it must be

The Problems of Sex

a union of spirits also and, if there is none or little, the bodily union fails to satisfy. Because it fails to satisfy, it creates the very frustration that modern men and women so greatly dread. The unsatisfied and frustrated will not believe that their unsatisfaction is due to their seeking satisfaction where it cannot be found. They only seek it more frequently and more strangely. They try many ways and many partners. They make constancy at last simply impossible for themselves, while at the same time remaining unsatisfied and at last sceptical about the very possibility of satisfaction.

Yet our race has not failed to produce lovers of a constancy so perfect that even the most convinced preachers of promiscuity cannot deny them the homage of admiration—or, if they do, they do not persuade the world to deny it. The great romances of the world are romances of faithful love. If it be objected that these are by no means always married lovers, it must be admitted; but the fact remains that it is their fidelity to each other that has moved the love and won the homage of the world. There is no inspiration, there is no romance, in light love.

Those therefore who would live nobly will attempt the heights of faithful love and, if its fulfilment is not possible for them for some reason they cannot disregard, they will be loyal to their ideal in celibacy.

Have women a special responsibility in all this? They have the special responsibility of special knowledge. They know even better than men the need of a settled home for children. They should therefore neither wreck their own home nor the home of other children. They will not accept any theory of marriage which weakens character and dissipates self-control beforehand. They

137

will not easily accept defeat. They will know that children need not only a stable *house* but a stable *home*, for their wants are psychological as well as physiological —as ours are.

Discussion about sex questions has become an intolerable bore to many of us. I do not dream of writing a book to add to the intolerable deal of writing on the subject. Nevertheless, it is too important to be forgotten by any writer on the subject of our future as a race. I speak of it here, however, chiefly to call attention to the fact that the attempt to find an easy way of life in this as in all things is utterly futile. There is no easy way. Let us not waste our time in looking for it. Let us rather look for the noblest, the fittest and the highest way, and then set about finding how to walk in it, with gentleness to all who make mistakes—even to ourselves.

I believe that if the sex relations of the future are governed by these principles, they will work themselves out in a right way. Celibacy, marriage, divorce, birth control and a multitude of delicate personal adjustments—all are involved in the question of sex. Some are suitable matters for legislation, some for the less formal but often even more binding operation of public opinion; some are utterly beyond such crude devices and can be adjusted only by the persons concerned. All should be guided towards a solution which respects the rights of children and their need for a stable home. All should recognize the beauty and dignity of sexual passion. None should act as though it were the most important thing in marriage or in life. None should suppose that life, in marriage or without it, childless or prolific, is or ever can be easy. It is hard and noble, or it is hard and ignoble: but always it is hard.

Chapter VIII

The Christian Basis of Civilization

WOMEN are more personal than men. They are sure to be, for their lives are more concerned with people than with any other interest, and these people of theirs are not "the masses" but individuals. Men fight in war, and their fight is one of nation against nation or class against class: the women's battle is a battle of one woman for one life—that of her child. In this warfare not death but life is the prize, and it is an individual life.

When, however, women are said to be more personal in their outlook than men, it is generally accepted— and intended—as a reproach. Why? If people are important, it is a good thing that half the race should think so. If they are more important than anything else, it should be a tribute rather than a reproach to say that women feel them to be so. In any case, since the coming of the totalitarian State has shown us what horrors can be brought about by contempt for individual freedom, and since mass production has shown itself to have grave disadvantages even in a democracy, women should be ready to declare their interest in individuals with all the strength they have. The world needs their message.

To proclaim this message belongs not to women only but to Christians everywhere. The infinite worth of the individual in the sight of God, as revealed by Jesus Christ, is the true basis of democracy. It used to be

Women's Partnership in the New World

said that if only one man on earth had sinned, God Almighty would have thought it worth while to be crucified for that man. This is democracy.

It is in part because this was what our Saviour taught and felt that his teaching has made so profound an appeal to women.

There are other reasons. Christ's attitude to women was one which, by its reverence for their personality, drew from them a passionate response. But this too was based on reverence for *all* personality and embraced women, slaves, criminals and outcasts in its glorious love.

Women who are mothers of other women, and of slaves, criminals and outcasts, share in their own more limited way his sense of the value of the human soul. "I could not love him, but his mother did" was the cry put into the mouth of a wife most hideously abused by her husband.* Browning knew a great deal about women when he made a woman say that. Mothers may indeed forget the children they bear, but very hardly. The life they gave cost too much to be despised, hated or forgotten.

In that new world to which we look with longing eyes the basis of democracy must be reverence for the human soul. It will embrace millions who are not Christians in name. There will be Moslems, Hindus, Confucians, Buddhists, Jews, and each great faith will bring its own gift to our world-wide civilization. The gift of the Christian is this: that all men and women everywhere are precious in the sight of God, and that "God would think it worth while to be crucified" for even one, and that one a sinner. There can be no

* Pompilia in *The Ring and the Book*, by Robert Browning.

The Christian Basis of Civilization

uniformity in institutions or governments, no one scheme of things for all men everywhere. Let each people make its own form of government, its own institutions. If there is one basis for all—reverence for personality—all the rest will come right.

Women to whom your Saviour made appeal as no other great Founder of religion has done, and who have responded to it as to no other, witnessing as evangelists, dying as martyrs for your faith, now is the hour for you to witness once again. In every aspect of it your age-old experience of life has fitted you for the task. As life-bearers, as the guardians of children, the makers of homes, as newcomers in world affairs, as long-sufferers of violence you had no power to resist, as the world's drudges, as the half-worshipped mothers of men, as souls for whom Christ died, as saints who died for him, give now to a sick and fainting world what you best can give—new hope, new life.

Index

143

For Product Safety Concerns and Information please contact our EU
representative GPSR@taylorandfrancis.com
Taylor & Francis Verlag GmbH, Kaufingerstraße 24, 80331 München, Germany